BLOODY B[...]SH HISTORY

SUFFOLK

ROBERT LEADER

ABOUT THE AUTHOR

Robert Leader is a photojournalist who has written and illustrated guidebooks to Cambridgeshire, Essex, Suffolk and Norfolk. His books for The History Press include *Bloody British History: Bury St Edmunds*, *Exploring Historical Essex* and *Exploring Historical Cambridgeshire*. He also writes crime, espionage and fantasy fiction and is the author of more than sixty published novels. For more, see:

www.robertleaderauthor.com

First published in 2014

The History Press
The Mill, Brimscombe Port
Stroud, Gloucestershire, GL5 2QG
www.thehistorypress.co.uk

British Library Cataloguing in Publication Data.
A catalogue record for this book is available from the British Library.

ISBN 978 0 7509 6149 3

Typesetting and origination by The History Press
Printed in Great Britain

CONTENTS

INTRODUCTION

OKAY, SO YOU'VE NOTICED that this book is a bit slim for a fully detailed history of Suffolk. That's because it isn't the complete history. It's called *Bloody British History: Suffolk* because that is what it is. It's all the bloody, gory bits, with all the dreary, boring bits left out.

It's not designed for classrooms and history lessons. It isn't going to teach you all the dry old stuff and turn you into a knowledgeable bore. It's just an enjoyable romp through all the blood and battles and all that's gory, ghoulish and bizarre.

It includes the legends, the murders and a few naughty bits. It may chill your blood, it may make you shudder, but once you're hooked, it won't let you get away. Read it if you dare.

NB All uncredited images are the property of the author.

Bibliography

Dymond, David and Northeast, Peter, *A History of Suffolk* (Phillimore, 1995)

Riching, Derek and Rudderham, Roger Ian, *Robber Barons and Fighting Bishops* (Jack Nichals Publications, 2003)

West, H. Mills, *Ghosts of East Anglia* (Barbara Hopkinson, 1984)

Wilson, Derek, *A Short History of Suffolk* (Batsford, 1977)

Borough of St Edmundsbury Official Guide, 1976

AD 61

AMBUSH ON THE STOUR

HISTORY IS A blood-spattered litany of lessons never learned and the history of Suffolk is no exception. No doubt the Stone Age men fought each other over the most attractive women, the best caves to live in and the spoils of the hunt. The Celtic tribes, though, enjoyed many a scrap on a larger scale. They developed iron-tipped spears and arrows to make the job of killing and butchering a bit easier than with the old flint axes.

The Iron Age peoples built wooden forts and dug ditches for their defence and, to scare the hell out of their enemies, painted their faces with blue woad and spiked their hair with white lime. They had developed the wheel and their nobles rode chariots with iron-rimmed wheels and flashing iron blades sticking out from the axles. Their priests were the white-robed Druids who worshipped the old gods of the earth, the moon and the water.

Then the Romans appeared in a full-scale invasion and we get the beginnings of recorded history.

The expanding Roman Empire launched its first attack upon the shores of England in the year 55 BC, which was led by Julius Caesar, who was then the Roman commander in Gaul. His eighty ships were beaten back by a combination of storms and dogged counter-attacks by the local Celtic tribes. One year later, Caesar returned with 800 ships and achieved some initial success. However, it was not until AD 43 that the Emperor Claudius personally led a major invasion of Britain.

The Emperor Claudius, from a contemporary coin. (THP)

The Roman army landed again in Kent and quickly defeated the local tribes, the Catuvellauni, under their king, Caratacus. They then marched north through Essex to what is now Colchester, where another ten tribal chiefs surrendered and signed treaties of friendship with Rome. They included the Iceni, or Eceni, who were then dominant in Suffolk and Norfolk.

The southern boundary of the Iceni tribal lands ran in a rough line from Newmarket to Aldeburgh, so the Iceni ruled most of Northern Suffolk. The southern half was the home of a Celtic tribe called the Trinovantes, but they had been invaded and conquered by the Catuvellauni from the west. The Iceni had long been rivals of the Catuvellauni and were happy to see their aggressive southern neighbours humbled and beaten.

The Roman invasion of Britain was prompted by two main causes: the Emperor Claudius needed a major victory to promote his position at home, but also found it necessary to control, invigorate and expand the trade in English corn and iron and cloth to sustain his large standing armies on the Rhine and in other parts of central Europe.

Roman map of Britain. (THP)

The Romans came, they saw, they conquered – but not without some initial setbacks. In AD 47, the Iceni joined a rebellion with the other Celtic tribes and that had to be put down, but it was only a foretaste of what was to happen in the traumatic year of AD 61.

Prasutagus – the client king of the Iceni – died, but in an effort to preserve some of his heritage and appease his Roman masters, his will left his estate

TARANIS, THE GOD OF WAR

Every Iceni village would have contained a Hall of Warriors, a general meeting place where the men would have gathered to drink and tell stories, and close by would be the temple of Taranis, the Celtic God of War.

Taran was the Iceni word for thunder, and the Celtic belief stated that the sound of thunder was the sound of Taranis' chariot wheels crushing the skulls of his enemies as he stormed through the sky. The chariot wheel was the god's symbol and has since become incorporated into the familiar symbol of the Celtic cross.

divided. One half was to go to Rome, the other half to his widow and heirs. The greedy Romans wanted it all and when Queen Boudicca protested, she was whipped and her two daughters were assaulted. In doing so, the Romans had enraged a tigress. Up until this point, the proud Iceni had pragmatically accepted the brute fact of Roman rule, but whipping their queen and abusing their princesses was something they could not tolerate.

Boudicca's cries for vengeance roused both her own people and the neighbouring Trinovantes. Suddenly the whole of East Anglia was united in an unholy uproar. Riding at the head of her racing hordes and chariots, the warrior queen stormed down upon the nearest symbol of Roman authority, the Roman town of Camulodunum, or what is now Colchester in Essex.

With their blue-painted faces and white, spiked hair, the blood-lusting Britons must have made a terrifying sight. The town was destroyed by fire and its inhabitants massacred. The great Temple to Claudius, who was worshipped as both emperor and god, was torn down. Much later, in 1907, the severed stone head of the once-revered statue of Claudius was fished out of the River Alde in Suffolk.

Boudicca still rides above Westminster Bridge.

Boudicca's enraged forces were unstoppable. The Ninth Legion, who had been stationed in the Nene Valley, marched south to deal with the insurrection. They were ambushed somewhere in the Valley of the Stour, probably near modern Haverhill, and lost 1,000 men.

The historical record is sparse on details, but to achieve her victory, Boudicca's attack must have come as a complete surprise. We can imagine her horse-drawn chariots bursting out of the trees like thunderbolts of fury as they smashed through the long column of weary, marching soldiers. To have lost so many men, the Romans would have had no time to form a shield wall or any of their usual defensive tactics. The snorting, foaming horses would have kicked through their lines, the wheel blades of the chariots slicing into the bare legs below the leather kilts of the soldiers. Many of them would have fallen crippled, to be speared where they lay by the following horde of screaming Britons.

The triumphant Boudicca led her forces on to the major Roman towns at London and then to St Albans, torturing and burning and slaughtering every Roman and Roman sympathiser she could find. The Iceni advance was only halted when the Romans managed to gather 10,000 troops to fight a set battle. The Romans were outnumbered ten to one but, at last, their superior training and discipline won the day. This time it was Boudicca's forces who were routed and slaughtered. The Warrior Queen is said to have taken poison and died by her own hand.

The reprisals in Suffolk and Norfolk were equally savage, and probably the reason for that stone head of Claudius to be thrown into the river. No survivor of the Iceni warriors would want to be caught with a trophy from the sacking of Camulodunum.

THE ROMAN SHORE FORTS

The next two centuries in Norfolk and Suffolk were relatively peaceful. The Roman economy and rule of law were comfortably accepted, along with the benefits of increased long-distance trade. The Iron Age landscape of hill forts, small settlements and farms was changed into one of expanding small Roman towns, small to luxury villas, often with underfloor heating and bath houses, and a growing network of arrow-straight Roman roads.

By the third century of Roman rule, the short, direct trade routes to Europe were being threatened by Saxon pirates, prompting the construction of a chain of Roman forts to defend the Suffolk shore. A large fort at Burgh protected the great estuary of converging rivers that has now shrunk to Breydon Water. Another fort at Walton near Felixstowe protected the estuary of the Orwell and the Stour.

The Roman war galleys attached to the forts patrolled the river mouths and the North Sea, fighting off the raids of Germanic pirates. But the Roman Empire was disintegrating and the barbarians grew bolder. When the Romans withdrew, it was the turn of the Saxons to invade the Suffolk shore.

AD 616

'AND THE RIVER RAN FOUL ...'

WHEN THE ROMANS marched their legions out of Suffolk and Norfolk in the early part of the fifth century, their departure marked the beginning of the power vacuum that became known as the Dark Ages. The Saxon pirates had already become a troublesome presence in the North Sea, and it was around this time that all the East Anglian defences broke down: the Saxon shore forts which the Romans had built at Burgh and Walton fell into decline. Stalwart Roman legionnaires no longer manned their ramparts. The fast-

Invaders from the sea harassed the region in this era. (THP)

response cavalry units had disappeared. The sleek Roman war galleys that had patrolled the vulnerable estuaries and river mouths of the Wash, the Yare and the Orwell had all gone.

Rome needed all she had to defend the heartland of a shrinking empire. In Rome's hour of need, Britain was abandoned. The pirates became bolder and in their wake came waves of Jutes and Angles and Saxons from the Germanic tribes of Northern Europe. Expanding communities and their ambitious warlords rowed their longboats across the North Sea and pushed their way bloodily into the estuaries and up the rivers. These people stayed as settlers and invaders, pushing back or mingling with the Celtic Britons. The newcomers were mainly illiterate. Like the Celtic peoples of the earlier Iron Age, they left no records to speak for themselves and so their first two centuries were a Dark Age. There would have been many bloody battles for supremacy between the established Roman Britons and the new arrivals, but we can again only imagine the fury and the despair of those engagements.

Slowly the Dark Ages were followed by the Saxon Age, when these intermingled peoples began to form powerful kingdoms. To the south were the kingdoms of Essex, Sussex, Wessex and Kent, and to the west and north, the kingdoms of Mercia and Northumbria. The Kingdom of East Anglia was formed by the North Folk and the South Folk and by the eastern part of Cambridgeshire. Its legendary symbol of three crowns is still used in the arms of the Borough of St Edmundsbury and the University of East Anglia.

The Venerable Bede, a monk historian writing around AD 730, listed Raedwald of East Anglia as one of the four major Over-Kings of the seventh century. His capital was at Rendlesham on the banks of the River Deben in the heart of Suffolk.

BEOWULF

This was the age of Beowulf, the legendary hero and leader of a band of warrior brothers whose courage and adventures were acclaimed in one of the few great poems of the time. Beowulf battled monsters and dragons. He slew the monster Grendel with his bare hands and then fought and killed the monster's mother in a cavern under a lake. He was a paragon of Saxon virtues and master of the Saxon sword. One suggestion is that the saga of Beowulf was actually written by a poet at the royal court of Raedwald. The story would have been sung and applauded in Raedwald's hall and in the lesser halls of the villages and settlements.

These were very closely knit tribal communities where social cohesion was based on kinship and honour and loyalty foremost to the king or lord. Personal security lay in knowing that relatives would avenge one's death and, in battle, all honour lay in protecting the chief. To survive the war leader or withdraw before him from the fight meant undying shame and disgrace.

The fictional Beowulf exemplified all these ideals and would have been a role model for every aspiring young Saxon hero.

SUTTON HOO

Much of what we know about the life and times of Raedwald was uncovered at Sutton Hoo, a high bluff overlooking the River Deben near Woodbridge in Suffolk. In 1939, in the largest of the seventeen burial mounds located here, a local archaeologist discovered the burial ship of an ancient Anglo-Saxon warrior king. It was one of the richest Anglo-Saxon graves ever to be excavated in Europe and the warrior king is believed to have been Raedwald. A great hoard of gold, bronze and silver was placed with him, along with his weapons and armour in his full-sized wooden burial ship, which was then covered by a massive earth barrow.

A similar ship burial was excavated near the River Alde and at a Saxon cemetery near Lakenheath two Saxon warriors have been unearthed, both of whom had their horses buried beside them. It seems that all kings and lords were buried with evidence of their wealth and power, and all warriors with their swords and shields to hand.

Sutton Hoo is now a National Trust site with a brand new exhibition hall to display its discoveries and to tell the story of how our Anglo-Saxon forebears once lived.

The recreated Saxon village at West Stow.

The three crowns of Saxon East Anglia.

At one stage, in AD 616, Raedwald gathered an army and marched it north through Mercia to do battle with Aethelfrid, the king of Northumbria. The story relates that Edwin, an exiled prince of Northumbria, had fled and sought sanctuary in Raedwald's royal court. Aethelfrid obviously saw Edwin as a dangerous rival and offered Raedwald bribes to have the young man murdered. Raedwald might have been tempted but his wife is credited with reminding him that he was a man of honour. The King of Northumbria then resorted to threats of war and invasion.

In these pagan days there were strict codes of honour. No true king or lord could sell his honour for money or betray the obligations of hospitality once given. Raedwald had sheltered Edwin and got himself into a fix with only one way out. He gathered his army and marched north to take the fight to Northumbria.

They met on the east bank of the River Idle and fought a ferocious battle. Raedwald had moved quickly, so that Aethelfrid had not had time to fully gather all his forces, although Raedwald lost his son Raegenhere in the battle. The East Anglian king had split his forces into three groups, led by himself, Raegenhere and Edwin. It seems that Aethelfrid may have mistaken Raegenhere for Edwin, and so he concentrated his assault on Raegenhere and cut him down. Raedwald was enraged at the death of his son and led a furious onslaught that resulted in a great slaughter of the Northumbrians, including the death of Aethelfrid. The East Anglian army smashed and butchered the Northumbrians and the river was said to have run foul with the blood of Englishmen.

Raedwald set the exiled prince Edwin upon the throne of Northumbria and returned to Suffolk in triumph. Now it was Aethelfrid's sons who had to take their turn in fleeing into exile.

AD 633

THE DEMON-BATTLING MONK

Saint Fursey, the man credited with converting the bulk of East Anglia to Christianity, was born in Ireland in the early seventh century. He was educated and then inducted into his uncle's monastery and devoted himself to a religious life. In his lifetime he established religious houses in Ireland, England and France, and was renowned for his Christ-like miracles and for his ecstatic visions.

He fell into trances, where he claimed to have heard heavenly choirs singing, recognised the saints and conversed with angels, who fought demons for his soul. He saw fantastic images of heaven

Burgh Castle, built by the Normans on the site of the old Roman shore fort and St Fursey's monastery.

and hell and received spiritual teaching and instructions, including a command to do twelve years of apostolic labour, and to 'Go, and announce the Word of God.' In one vision he passed through the fires of hell and a spiteful demon hurled the body of a burning sinner at him. The body struck and burned Fursey's flesh, and the saint is said to have carried the burn mark for the rest of his life.

Fursey faithfully fulfilled his twelve years of apostolic work, travelling the length and breadth of Ireland to spread the news of Christ and the Gospels, and then retired to a small island, where he founded his first monastery. However, the need to preach and spread the word beyond the shores of Ireland soon prevailed. Fursey gave up all of his material belongings and, with his two brothers and a small group of fellow monks, began his itinerant wandering.

Christianity had been first introduced to East Anglia by the Romans but was virtually washed away in the waves of subsequent human invasions. The Anglo-Saxons brought with them their own gods: the pagan Norse gods of later Scandinavian mythology, such as Tiw, Woden and Thor. We have them with us still, hidden in the day names of each week: Tuesday, Wednesday and Thursday.

However, Christianity came again in the seventh century, carried by dedicated monks like Fursey from Ireland and elsewhere in Europe. The faith reached southern and eastern England through the marriage of the Kentish King Ethelbert to a Frankish princess. Ethelbert became a Christian and on a royal visit to Suffolk, the great King Raedwald was persuaded to be baptised and to bring the Christian faith to East Anglia. However, the call of the pagan gods was still strong and while practising

BISHOP FELIX

Saint Fursey and Saint Felix, from a stained-glass window in Alpheton church.

A contemporary of Fursey was the French Bishop Felix, whom Sigeberht also welcomed into his court and established as the first Bishop of East Anglia. Felix built his church at Dummoc, which some scholars interpret as the old seaport of Dunwich, while others believe the site was at Walton. As both sites have now been obliterated, Dunwich by the fury of the sea and Walton buried under what is now Felixstowe, the actual location is unclear.

It seems that, despite their different backgrounds, the wild Irish monk and the Burgundian priest worked well together and a stained-glass window in the tiny church at Alpheton commemorates their meeting.

Felix was Bishop of East Anglia for seventeen years and, when he died, he too became a saint.

MISSION TO NEUSTRIA

Neustria was the western part of the Kingdom of the Franks, covering most of what is now Northern France between the rivers of the Loire and the Seine. Fursey's preaching mission led him to the village of Ponthieu, where he found the whole population in mourning as the young and only son of Duke Hayson, the lord of the area, had died. Fursey paid his respects and prayed over the body, and the boy was miraculously restored to life. Fursey performed other healing miracles and his fame preceded him to Peronne. Here he was offered a site for his monastery beside the beautiful River Marne.

Fursey built his monastery and three chapels. Eventually his two brothers returned to East Anglia and Fursey was eventually struck down while on his way back to England to rejoin them; it seems that he had some premonition of his impending death. By a strange coincidence he fell ill and died in the same town where he had raised the duke's son and so laid the joyous foundations for all his success.

his Christian faith, Raedwald prudently kept up his altars and his offerings to the old gods. In this unsettled age it was probably considered a good idea to hedge one's bets. To justify their rule Raedwald's family, the Wuffingas, had also claimed a direct lineage back to both Woden and Julius Caesar.

Christianity had to struggle hard against the entrenched power of the old gods, but eventually it was to replace them. Raedwald died and was eventually succeeded by Sigeberht, who was also a Christian. Sigeberht had already established the first East Anglian bishopric at Dommoc, somewhere in Suffolk, and it was Sigeberht who greeted Fursey and his wild-haired group of fellow monks when they arrived in around AD 633.

With the new king's blessing, the Irish missionaries established themselves at the site of the old Roman fort that was later to become Burgh Castle in Norfolk. Fursey founded an abbey, which has since disappeared, and laboured to convert the Picts and Saxons.

Fursey's benefactor Sigeberht was killed in a battle with King Pemba of Mercia, but the new King Anna and his Saxon nobles continued their support for the Christian mission. Finally Fursey felt that the foundation of his work was accomplished. He retired for another year of rest and then took to the road again with his brothers to travel into France, there to found another monastery and to continue his task of preaching and converting others to the Christian faith. He performed more miracles, including the raising of a duke's son from the dead, and was obviously a very charismatic preacher and healer.

Saint Fursey died around AD 650, from an illness incurred while he was again travelling in France. His body lay unburied for a month, waiting for the dedication of the church where it was to be interred. For those thirty days it lay incorrupt, attracting pilgrims from all over France, and was reported as giving off a sweet odour.

AD 794

AETHELBERHT LOSES HIS HEAD

RAEDWALD WAS PERHAPS the first English king to dominate all the other Anglo-Saxon kingdoms, but after his death in around AD 625 the power struggles continued. Eventually the kingdom of Mercia rose to prominence under the warrior king Pemba who was a bloody-fisted, old-fashioned pagan. Sigeberht, the son of Raedwald and the new king of the East Angles, and Edwin, Raedwald's protégée who still ruled Northumbria, were both Christian kings. There was plenty of scope there for more bloody warfare, which Pemba pursued with ruthless determination.

Edwin got the chop at the Battle of Hatfield Chase.

Sigeberht tried to give it all up and retired to the small monastery he had built at Beodricsworth. He took the robe and cowl and became a monk, devoting his life to prayer. Or so he thought. Pemba was in a conquering mood and, in AD 636, the pagan king of Mercia invaded East Anglia. The warriors of Suffolk grabbed their spears and mustered to meet the challenge, but they had no confidence in their new king Ecgric. A bunch of them decided that they needed a holy man in their vanguard to show that the new Christian god was on their side.

Sigeberht was the obvious choice, their ex-king who had now taken all his vows. They went to fetch him but Sigeberht was reluctant to leave the shelter of his monastery. Eventually his desperate subjects hauled him off to the battlefield anyway, still wearing his monk's habit. They probably hoped that the mere sight of the holy man in their ranks would inspire a bit of hope in the local lads and frighten off the beastly pagans.

The pagans were not impressed. They charged into bloody battle and slaughtered the East Anglians.

Sigeberht had refused to forsake his vows, but by all accounts he was no coward. He refused to wear armour or wield a weapon of war, but he went into the fight wielding a big stick. Sadly, faith and a stick were not enough to smite the heathen. Sigeberht was killed and so was Ecgric.

Pemba had conquered East Anglia but he couldn't be everywhere at once. He found a pliable nephew of Raedwald's called Anna who he set up as Mercia's vassal king of East Anglia. Anna managed to stay on the throne as a figurehead king until he upset his overlord in AD 654. Suddenly Pemba and his Mercian hordes were again marching in full force upon their eastern neighbour. Anna tried to put up a fight and defend the Devil's Dyke, but the Mercians stormed his defences through a hail of spears and breached his shield wall. They flooded through and chased Anna and his warriors right across Suffolk, until they were trapped at Blythborough with their backs to the sea. Another slaughter robbed East Anglia of another king: Anna and most of his followers were all killed. At least four kings of East Anglia are said to have died in battles with Mercia.

The historical records tend to be a bit sketchy in the century that followed, but it seems that by AD 794 Aethelberht, who claimed a lineage of descent from the great Raedwald, was then the king of East Anglia. A king named Offa had become the king of still-dominant Mercia.

It seems that Aethelberht was intending to marry Offa's daughter, which was probably not a love match but would have been seen as politically expedient. He journeyed to Offa's royal villa at Sutton Walls in Hertfordshire to become acquainted with his intended bride, but he was not the only one who was reluctant to see the nuptials take place. Offa's wife Cynehtrith, often referred to as an evil queen, tried to have him poisoned and – when that failed – persuaded her husband to have him murdered. The unlucky Aethelberht was bound and beheaded. One account states that Offa, King of Mercia, ordered the head of Aethelberht, King of East Anglia, to be struck off. Another claims that while the remains were being removed, the head rolled off a cart and fell into a ditch. There it restored the sight of a blind man who was passing, which ensured that Aethelberht came to be venerated as a saint.

These were perilous times, especially for kings.

DEVIL'S DYKE

The earth rampart of Devil's Dyke.

It was possibly during Raedwald's reign that the massive earthwork known as Devil's Dyke was reinforced to form the western boundary of the East Anglian kingdom. In places 11 metres high, this great earth wall can still be seen today, running for 7 miles from Reach to Wooditton in Cambridgeshire. The original ditch and rampart goes back much further in time but it is known to have been re-established during this period.

This massive man-made barrier filled the gap between the thick Breckland forests and the wet fenland marshes. King Anna is known to have defended it in an attempt to prevent the army of Mercia invading his kingdom, but his forces failed against superior ferocity and numbers.

AD 865

VICIOUS VIKINGS

AFTER THE PAGAN incursions of the bloody kings of Mercia, things finally calmed down as the many monks inhabiting England converted most of the country to Christianity. Trade improved and towns, farms and settlements expanded. Life was easier. East Anglia was divided along the river line of the Waveny and Suffolk and Norfolk began to be seen as the separate counties they are today. The good Saxon folk of Suffolk planted their crops, tended their animals, said their prayers and built more monasteries and churches, and probably thought that the worst of history was behind them.

Then, seemingly out of nowhere, the Vikings came. A single sail would appear from the wastes of the cold North Sea. The sails would multiply until a fleet of deadly longships would become visible, powering over the waves with the wind behind them and rows of fearsome warriors pulling lustily at the double banks of oars.

A recreation of a Viking longship. (Wikimedia)

They would hit the coastal towns, or surge up the Orwell or the Stour to attack the inland settlements. As their boats struck the beach or the riverbank, the Vikings would drop their oars and snatch up swords and axes and steel helmets. Bounding ashore, they would burn and plunder, although not necessarily in that order. Usually they would butcher all the fighting men first. They kept this up for fifty years, often looting monasteries, which they quickly found were ripe for the taking. The holy places were full of treasures and the monks too slow and feeble to defend them. A good monk clasped his hands in prayer and waited for the executioner's axe to fall, or fled squealing and was easily cut down from behind. The Viking butchers rarely lost a casualty and it was all good fun.

At the same time, they were testing and probing the strengths and weaknesses of the local Saxon warlords. Finally, they decided that the whole island was ready and waiting for a suitable conqueror. In the wake of all the small-scale pirate raids, a character called Ivar the Boneless brought a full-scale army across the North Sea and landed on the Suffolk shore.

The terrified Saxons fled before the invasion. Usually they were able to return after a few days, but this time the Vikings did not settle for a little marauding and then return to their boats. This time, the Danish Army was here to stay.

The king of East Anglia now was the boy king Edmund. The Vikings were vicious and powerful and Edmund's forces were relatively weak. Discretion seemed the better part of valour, and so Edmund saw no choice but to negotiate and agree the terms of a treaty. Edmund gave the Danes free passage and horses, and in return they agreed not to attack his lands. It allowed the invaders to spend the winter at Thetford, just across the River Ouse in what is now Norfolk.

This breathing space enabled the Norsemen to bring in more reinforcements and consolidate their position. When spring came they headed inland, north and west to attack and loot the neighbouring kingdoms of Northumbria and Mercia.

No doubt Edmund and his people were glad to see them go, but it was only a short respite and within a couple of years, the Viking's came back. They spent another winter at Thetford and then used their camp there to launch attacks on the farms and monasteries of East Anglia. They had broken the treaty and Edmund could no longer stand by and do nothing. He gathered his forces and, in AD 887, confronted his enemies in a pitched battle. It was a merciless fight, said to have lasted from 'dawn till dusk until the stricken field was red with the blood of the countless numbers who perished' (according to Roger of Wendover). In the end, Edmund was defeated and was forced to flee from the field with what remained of his scattered army. He was finally caught and cruelly tortured by the pagan Vikings, who demanded that he renounce his Christian faith. Edmund refused and the Danes tied him to a tree and shot him full of arrows. Finally they lost patience and chopped off his head.

The latest statue of St Edmund stands on a town centre roundabout.

Edmund, King of East Anglia, killed by the Danes. (Wikimedia)

Edmund's friends later found his body. Finding the head was a bit more difficult, but eventually the head itself called out to them from the thicket where it had been thrown. There the severed head was being guarded and cradled in the paws of a huge female wolf. The wolf stood up and walked away, as though it knew its job was done. When placed at the neck of the body, the head miraculously reattached itself, all the wounds healed and the body never corrupted. Edmund was declared a saint and was eventually enshrined in Sigeberht's small monastery at Beodricsworth, which was eventually to become the great abbey of St Edmundsbury.

The ruins of St Edmund's shrine at Bury St Edmunds.

A SUCCESSION OF SAINTS

Edmund was the third Saxon king to die a gruesome death and then become venerated as a saint. Edwin, who Raedwald placed on the throne of Northumbria, was declared a saint after his death at the Battle of Hatfield Chase. Edwin had converted to Christianity and destroyed his pagan temple and all its idols, which meant that his death in battle with the pagans ensured him his sainthood.

Aethelberht was another Christian king murdered by the pagans, so he too became a saint.

The particularly gruesome manner of Edmund's execution, plus his repeated refusals to denounce his Christian faith, ensured him the supremacy among saints. His shrine at Bury St Edmunds became a great centre of pilgrimage. In terms of size, wealth and prestige, it was one of the five most important abbeys in England and played a pivotal role in the growth of the town of Bury St Edmunds and the history of Suffolk.

AD 1010

ULFKETEL, THE FIGHTING EARL

IT WAS LEFT to another English king, Alfred the Great, King of Wessex, to finally halt this first invasion of the Danes. In AD 878, Alfred won a major battle at Edington in Wiltshire and forced a treaty on their leader, Guthrum. The Danes were too numerous to be driven back over the North Sea, but the treaty limited their expansion to East Anglia. Suffolk became one of the counties where the Danelaw prevailed.

The Danelaw lasted well into the next century. The rich soils of Suffolk were a vast improvement on their wild and barren homelands and so many of the men who came as pirates and soldiers of fortune stayed as settlers and farmers and their families and friends came to join them. Gradually they were assimilated into the local Saxon communities.

Alfred was another Christian king and as part of the treaty forged at Edington, Guthrum and several of his captains were baptised as Christians. Many of the new pagan settlers also accepted the new religion and, ironically, many of the descendants of the butchers who had caused the martyrdom of St Edmund eventually came share his faith and worship at his shrine.

Over 100 years passed before the Viking assaults began again. Ethelred was the new king of England and he tried to pay off the raiders with the tribute that became known as the Danegeld. The bribes failed and every year the raiders kept returning. In desperation Ethelred ordered the infamous St Brice's Day Massacre, the ethnic cleansing of every Dane in England. One of those killed was the sister of the Danish king

Massacre of the Danes on St Brice's Day. (THP)

Sweyn Forkbeard and, in AD 1004, Sweyn led another full-scale invasion of East Anglia.

Ipswich had been sacked in 991, followed by the Battle of Maldon, when the Essex men under Earl Brythnoth had been defeated. Now Sweyn and his fleet of ravaging longships moved up the Suffolk coast, burned Ipswich again and penetrated the Yare to Norwich, which they also looted and burned. They swung back toward Suffolk and sacked Thetford on the River Ouse.

Enter Ulfketel the Brave, the Saxon Earl of East Anglia. He was possibly of part-Danish descent from those original settlers but was true to his homeland. He is said to have married Wulfhild, who was a daughter of King Ethelred the Unready and a sister of Edmund Ironside, who succeeded Ethelred as king. Ulfketel raised a Saxon army and succeeded in stopping the Vikings and chasing them back to their ships. He ordered the ships to be burned but the raiders escaped before the order could be carried out.

In AD 1010, the longships were back again under Thorkill the Tall for a repeat performance. Ipswich and Norwich were again sacked. Earl Ulfketel bought a truce after the sack of Norwich, but Sweyn double-crossed him and sailed off to put Thetford once more to the axe and sword.

Unlucky Thetford, like Ipswich and Norwich, had also been a repeated target for the Danes; about 100 years before, the great army that had defeated and killed Edmund had made their winter quarters there. King Sweyn had already raided it in AD 1004 and now, in AD 1010, he burned the town to the ground.

Enraged Ulfketel followed and fought a bloody battle in which many more East Anglians were killed. Over 14,000 men were said to have been involved in this particular bloodbath at Ringmere and the dead of both sides lay thick upon the ground. This time the Danes were victorious and the Saxons lost the day, although even the Vikings conceded that they had never met harder swordplay than Ulfketel had brought them.

ST EDMUND'S LANCE

King Sweyn Forkbeard died outside the walls of Bury St Edmunds. His forces had besieged the town, demanding a huge ransom if they were to leave it unravaged. Suddenly the Danish king began screaming in pain or terror and collapsed as though struck by an invisible bolt of lightning.

Legend says that he saw Saint Edmund the Martyr riding at him from the clouds on a white horse, and that Edmund speared him through the heart with a silver lance. These were the words he screamed as he died. Either Sweyn had a heart attack and his own fears and superstitions overwhelmed him, or the saint had appeared in the town's time of need to defend his shrine.

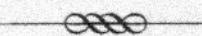

Now the Vikings were free to ravage all of Suffolk, which they did with a vengeance. In their hunt for booty, they also had to eat and they slaughtered all the cattle and sheep they could find for meat. Like starving wolves they devoured everything that was edible and, when they had devastated the lands of Suffolk, they moved down into Essex. Ulfketel had rallied his remaining warriors again and pursued them to Ashingdon Hill to join with the English king for a final bloody battle. Here Ulfketel the fighting Earl of Suffolk was finally killed.

All English efforts failed, and Ethelred finally fled to France. By AD 1017 Sweyn's son, the Danish monarch King Canute, was also king of all England. For administrative purposes, Canute divided his new kingdom into four earldoms, one of which was the Earldom of East Anglia. For the rest of his reign, Suffolk and Norfolk were ruled by a Danish Earl.

The Danish royal line ended two years after the death of King Canute, and the royal line of Wessex was restored. Edward the Confessor became king, but there was still the thorny and familiar problem of succession. The Danes still believed they had a claim, and so did the Normans.

1066

The 1066 Viking invasion of England was not by the Danes, but by the Norwegians. A Norse army under King Harald Hardrada of Denmark landed in Northumbria in 1066 and sacked the great city of York. Harold of Wessex, the last Saxon king, marched north to meet them. His army defeated the Norsemen and left thousands of them dead at the Battle of Stamford Bridge.

But 1066 was a fateful year. While Harold dealt with one challenge and emerged triumphant, a fleet of seventy ships under William the Conqueror had landed on the Sussex coast. Harold's army turned south and marched to meet them, covering 200 miles in five days.

A Victorian view of the Battle of Hastings – the moment when Harold fell. (THP)

On the high ground of a ridge, the exhausted English army formed up behind their traditional battle line of over-lapping shields. They faced three separate lines of Norman archers, Norman infantry and mounted Norman knights. Under hails of arrows and the charges of the knights the Saxon shield wall held all day, but it eventually broke and a fatal arrow struck King Harold in the eye.

The glory of Anglo-Saxon England died on the field at Hastings and the Viking age had also come to an end. The age of the Normans had begun.

AD 1069

THE LAST VIKING ASSAULT ON IPSWICH

IPSWICH WAS FIRST called Gypeswic, meaning a settlement on the Gipping. It was first established in early Saxon times on the left bank of the river, where it enters the wider seawater estuary of the Orwell. A few farms merged into a small trading centre and it was probably the Wuffinga dynasty that built the first crude landing stages for ships. Gypeswic was ideally situated to receive trade from the Rhine and from Scandinavia. Unfortunately, it was also ideally situated to receive the recurring waves of Viking raiders.

In the ebb and flow of Viking attacks and invasions, Gypeswic was occupied or plundered many times. In 869, it was again captured by the Danes when ninety-three dragon ships surged up the Orwell, their black sails filling the whole width of the river and the mighty swish of a thousand oars joining with

Alfred the Great aboard the English ships, exhorting the Saxons to resist the Vikings. (THP)

A REBELLIOUS KNIGHT

The Norman knight who stopped the last Viking incursion into East Anglia was Ralph Guarder. He earned the Conqueror's favour and William gratefully made him the Earl of East Anglia, bringing Suffolk and Norfolk together again under the same jurisdiction. He was given Norwich Castle, which the Conqueror had founded himself.

However, William and his loyal knight soon fell out of harmony. Ralph had chosen a bride and the king refused to sanction the marriage, which would have joined two powerful families. William was desperate to avoid any power blocs large enough to compete with his own. William had briefly returned to Normandy, and Ralph was soon plotting a conspiracy behind his back.

However, one of Ralph's co-conspirators betrayed him to the Archbishop of Canterbury, whom William had left in charge of his English kingdom during his absence. A loyal army was raised, led by two bishops. Ralph's forces were beaten in battle and one of the bishops ordered that all captured rebels must have their right foot cut off as a punishment. These were ungodly bishops in ungodly times. Ralph was fortunate, in that he escaped the battlefield with two legs, and was forced to flee to Denmark.

Ralph found allies and soon returned with a fleet of 200 Danish ships to support his rebellion. By then King William had returned from France and, faced with the king's army, Ralph fled once more, and his Danish allies with him. Ralph left his wife to hold Norwich Castle, but after a three-month siege she surrendered.

Ralph finally went on the First Crusade, probably to atone for his many sins, and died on the road to Palestine.

Norwich Castle.

the battle cries of the hairy warriors. The Danes were here for another long stay and held the town for fifty years.

This was the time of the Danegeld, which bought an uneasy peace until Alfred the Great entered the pages of English history. Down in Wessex, Alfred started to build his own ships to combat the Danes. Alfred saw sea power as one way to defeat them and his plan was to intercept the northern raiding fleets before they could land on his southern coasts. He built his ships larger than the Viking longboats, so they could carry more armed men. They out-classed the Viking vessels at sea but, being larger and heavier, they were less manoeuvrable in the shallower waters of the inlets and estuaries.

However, in 884, Alfred's new fleet caught up with one of the Viking raiding fleets and chased them back to their homeport at Gypeswic. Battle raged in the double mouth of the Orwell and the Stour and bloody slaughter ensued. One tactic of this new form of warfare involved crashing alongside a fleeing ship, showering it with arrows as they closed, and then quickly lashing the two vessels together. Battle could then be joined in the traditional manner as the attacking force flowed on board the defending vessel, thrusting their shields before them and swinging their swords and axes.

Because Alfred's ships and crews were larger, the Vikings were outnumbered and once their ship was tethered, they could only dive overboard or fight to the death. They were Vikings and most of them died fighting. Alfred is said to have captured sixteen of the fleeing longships and butchered their crews, while many of their land-based comrades watched helplessly from the shore at Shotley on a headland that is still known as Bloody Point.

The Vikings had rebuilt and strengthened the old Saxon ramparts around Ipswich, but it was not enough for, in 917, the town was recaptured by the English. The Vikings returned in 991 for another assault, moving down into Essex where they fought the Battle of Maldon and again overthrew the Anglo-Saxon monarchy.

They were eventually thrown out again, but after the Battle of Hastings, the persistent pirates obviously felt that the Suffolk defences were in disarray and staged another assault on Ipswich in 1069. Again they were thrown back and this was their swansong; their last assault on Ipswich.

The Normans were in power now and they were consolidating their grip. The Norman knights who had been given their share of the English lands by William the Conqueror were building their castle strongholds all over England. These knights built a castle at Ipswich and rebuilt another at Walton to dominate the Stour and Orwell estuary.

Old Gipeswic was no longer a soft target. The new Ipswich was well defended.

AD 1174

BIGODS BOLD, THE BULLY BARONS

NORWICH CASTLE WAS next given to a knight named Roger Bigod, who had already been granted 117 Suffolk manors. Roger was the first of an infamous line of Norfolk barons and his son Hugh later built the first great Norman castles at Bungay and Framlingham. A tyrannical bully, by all accounts, Hugh not only terrorised the local Saxons, but frequently rebelled against his king, attacking the Royalist castles, surrendering, or changing sides, whichever became politically or militarily expedient. Generally he was successful in his rampaging, and it was said in his time that whoever wore the Crown in London, it was the Bigods who effectively ruled Suffolk.

Orford Castle. (Draco2008, www.flickr.com/people/draco2008)

Eventually Hugh Bigod provoked his king too far by supporting the sons of Henry II in an armed revolt. Henry set about containing his troublesome baron by building his own massive castle at Orford to control the approaches to Framlingham from the sea. Walton Castle had been a stronghold of the Bigods but it was confiscated and garrisoned by Henry in 1156. With the castles at Norwich, Eye, and Thetford also in Royalist hands, Hugh Bigod was trapped within a royal cordon.

Hugh hired French and Flemish mercenary troops and launched a defiant bid for independence. Immediately on landing with the Flemish army, Hugh's ally, the Earl of Leicester, attacked the castles at Walton and Eye but was repelled. However, the troops were

EYE CASTLE

In central Suffolk all the Saxon lands that had been held by Edric of Laxfield were given to the Norman knight William Malet, who was responsible for building the castle at Eye. Malet is believed to have died fighting against the forces of Hereward the Wake, the last defiant Saxon earl who had created a stronghold at the Isle of Ely in the Cambridgeshire Fens. Malet's son Robert took over his role of High Sherriff of Suffolk and helped to defeat the rebellion of Ralph Guarder.

Robert Malet seems to have fallen out of favour with William II, probably through befriending the wrong brother in the royal squabbles of the time. He disappeared from Suffolk for a while, probably dodging back to Normandy. The kings and barons of this particular period of medieval history were constantly intriguing and fighting on both sides of the Channel.

The castle mound and fragments of wall rise over the church tower at Eye.

Robert reappeared at the coronation of Henry I in 1100 and resumed his old offices in Suffolk and his occupation of Eye Castle. It was not for long and the castle was next confiscated by Henry II, who installed one of his own supporters.

As a royal castle, Eye was besieged by Hugh Bigod and his allies in 1173. This was a full-scale siege but the castle held. Eventually, the castle was sacked in the Second Barons' War of 1265, after surviving another attack and a second siege.

Bungay Castle.

able to totally destroy Haughley Castle, smoking out the defenders with burning brushwood stacked against the walls and pushing what was left of the castle into the moat. The surviving nobles were ransomed, but the common soldiers were brutally murdered by having their throats slit.

Ranulph de Broc, who commanded the castle, was killed in the fighting, but in his particular case it was felt that he had only received his just reward. Ranulph was one of the group of knights who had murdered Thomas Becket in Canterbury Cathedral. The ill-fated archbishop had infuriated the king by opposing his proposed reforms of the church. Henry had (supposedly) uttered the fateful words, 'Will no one rid me of this turbulent priest?' and the Suffolk knight and his friends had taken him at his word. Many people, therefore, saw Ranulph's subsequent murder as God's vengeance.

Retribution finally caught up with Leicester and his Flemish army in a bloody battle at Fornham St Genevieve, near Bury St Edmunds. Forces loyal to the king and rallying to the banner of St Edmund met and massacred the Flemings in the marshes beside the River Lark. Many of the Suffolk peasants and freemen who had been forced to hide and watch as their barns were plundered and their livestock slaughtered now had the opportunity to take their revenge. They joined the victors and, with flails and pitchforks, willingly helped to turn the grasslands red.

Robert de Beaumont, the Earl of Leicester, and his wife were captured, but Hugh Bigod escaped and fled back to his home refuge in Bungay. Soon after, Henry himself marched a royal army upon Framlingham and Bungay, where Hugh Bigod, the bane of Suffolk, at last surrendered.

AD 1216

THE BARONS' WAR

KING RICHARD THE Lionheart was the first English king to lead the Holy War in Palestine. He led the Third Crusade, continuing the repeated Christian efforts to recapture Jerusalem from the Saracens. This was an expensive business and it was Richard's desperate need for money to finance his crusades that enabled the Bigods, the rebellious Earls of Suffolk, to buy back their titles and rebuild their castles at Bungay and Framlingham.

When Richard died, his brother John became king. John managed to lose the

Barons swearing an oath to regain their liberties; Roger Bigod was one of these men. (THP)

entire French half of the old Norman Empire and quickly became involved in another civil war with his English barons. By this time another Roger Bigod ruled over the castles at Norwich, Framlingham and Bungay, and again a Bigod baron pitted his strength against his king.

This time, there was something useful in the outcome. This Roger Bigod was one of those barons who swore the oath that ultimately forced John to sign Magna Carta, the great charter that became the foundation of English government and law.

The abbey of St Edmundsbury became, on 20 November 1214, the secret meeting place for the barons and earls who had tired of the despotic behaviour of their arrogant king. Because the shrine was a magnet for pilgrims, and also because it was far enough removed from London to be safe from the king's spies, twenty-five of the most powerful men in the land assembled before the High Altar. They were there ostensibly to perform their religious duties as part of their pilgrimage on St Edmund's Day, but also to swear on their sacred oath, here in this holy place, that they would force their king to recognise and sign the Great Charter of Liberties that the Archbishop of Canterbury now presented before them.

The Great Act, or Magna Carta as it became known, set up the principles of British law, and the basic foundations for representative and constitutional government. True to their oath, the barons marched upon London and seized the city, forcing the recalcitrant King John to set his seal to the charter at Runnymede in June of the following year. So the shrine of the martyred king had also become the cradle of the law.

John's bad luck was to continue. The tricky king regarded his signature as just a way of buying time while he still attempted to scheme a way out of his

THE STENCH OF ROTTING CORPSES

The barons were not the only ones to seek help from France. King John hired an army of mercenaries from Poitou and another force from Flanders under the command of a man named Hugh de Bovas, who was supposed to land his men in Kent and from there link up with the king's forces.

But the cruel North Sea, Kipling's 'Old Grey Widow-Maker', usually had a will of its own. It had sunk the White Ship, drowning the heir of Henry II, which led directly to the civil war between Stephen and Matilda. Now with an equal disregard for the lofty schemes of kings, the weather played its hand again.

A sudden and terrible storm blew up and wrecked most of de Bovas' ships. Instead of a powerful force of fighting men landing strategically in Kent, more than 40,000 drowned bodies were washed up along the shores of Suffolk and Norfolk. They included the fish-nibbled remains of Hugh de Bovas. Along the whole of the coastline, the air was tainted with the stench of rotting corpses.

King John signs Magna Carta. (THP)

The right-hand pillar marks the site of the High Altar, where the barons swore their oath to enforce Magna Carta.

THE LAST BIGOD

In 1294, the fifth earl of the line was yet another Roger Bigod. The king on the throne in London was Edward I, but otherwise little had changed. The kings of England were still quarrelling with their cousins in France, and Edward was raising another army for yet another bloodletting jaunt in Gascony. He wanted Roger to take his Suffolk forces into the campaign and, like his troublesome predecessors, the current Roger Bigod again refused to bend to the royal will. Like true bullies, the Bigods only threw their weight around where they saw a clear profit and could be sure of winning. Edward himself was not going to be present on the campaign and so Roger claimed that he had no duty to be there either.

History records Edward roaring at the earl: 'By God, Earl, you will either go or hang.'

To which Bigod roared back: 'By God, King, I will neither go nor hang.' Bigod stormed out of the royal presence. He was still powerful enough to deny the king; he did not go and he did not hang but, after his death, his mighty castle at Framlingham was claimed by the Crown and fell into despair and ruin.

The Bigod reign was over and the dynasty disappeared from Suffolk history.

obligations. Realising that John meant to break their contract and had no real intention of implementing its reforms, the barons continued their rebellion.

The barons persuaded Louis of France to invade England in support of their cause. The king had to deal with the French first, but eventually he was able to turn his attention to the eastern barons. He marched his army to Framlingham, where Roger Bigod suddenly saw the error of his ways and surrendered without a fight. John went on to capture Ipswich and then turned down into Essex, where he suffered another reverse and had to retreat; the barons promptly reclaimed Suffolk. The luckless people of the countryside saw their fields, crops and livestock devastated as the armies moved to and fro.

Because he was surrounded by enemies, John kept his royal baggage train with him as he moved from town to town. Fleeing from Norfolk, he tried to take a short cut across The Wash and was caught by the incoming tide. He lost all of his treasure, including the Crown jewels, and barely escaped with his life. It was a short-lived escape, for John soon died of natural causes. The Bigods survived and remained in power as the ruling dynasty in Suffolk for another century.

AD 1326

THE SHE-WOLF OF FRANCE

THE ENGLISH CHANNEL WAS never wide enough and the cold grey waters of the North Sea were the invasion route for recurring waves of pirates and invaders from the continent of Europe. However, in the September of 1326, it was not the single square sails of Viking longships that grew ominously on the bleak horizon. Instead, the sails of eight French warships swiftly took shape. They landed with a fleet of smaller vessels on the Suffolk coast at Walton near the mouth of the Orwell.

Isabella, the She-Wolf of France. (Illustrated London News, *1935, THP)*

As the ships unloaded their small boats, they discharged a mercenary army led by Isabella, Queen of England, and her lover Roger Mortimer, one of the powerful lords of the Welsh Marches. The queen wore widow's black, although her husband, King Edward II, was still alive. For Isabella, the marriage was already dead.

Isabella was a daughter of Phillip IV of France. She had been married at the age of 12 to England's king in a political alliance that was never a love affair. The handsome, bisexual king had paid more attention to his male lovers, even though she had borne him four children. Her eldest son was with her now and she was determined to plant him on the throne as Edward III and rule through him as regent.

Her army was small – perhaps 1,500 fighting men – but once they had settled the tricky question of where exactly they had landed they moved swiftly, sweeping through Suffolk and heading for London. The time was ripe, for England had been crippled by bad harvests, cattle disease and drought. Edward II had proved a weak military leader, losing Scotland to Robert the Bruce and being forced to flee from the Battle of Bannockburn. Many of the English barons were again ready to rebel against their king, despising him for his romantic attachments to his male 'favourites'. The peasants were desperate for things to change. Insurrection was in the air.

Queen Isabella, better known to history as the She-Wolf of France, had chosen her moment well. As she led her forces inland, her army quickly gained size and momentum. Most of the local levies that were hastily organised in her path promptly changed sides and joined her at the first encounter. She stormed through Bury St Edmunds and then Cambridge, gathering up a couple of dissident earls and their forces on the way. Edward realised that she was unstoppable and fled from London with his lover Hugh Despenser the Younger before she arrived.

Isabella now commanded a massive coalition of all her husband's opponents, and kept up the pursuit. She chased Edward and Hugh into Wales, where they tried to escape in a small boat. Bad weather drove the boat ashore again and finally Isabella's forces captured the king and his paramour. Retribution was immediate and gruesome.

A CHOPPING BLOCK FOR THE ABBOT

The same patterns of economic collapse and general public unrest that paved the way for Isabella's seizing of the English throne also led to a crisis in the always prickly relationship between the good citizens of Bury St Edmunds and their rulers at the Great Abbey. Essentially it was a matter of who got the tax money that was extorted from everyone who passed through the town gates. The town burghers wanted a share and the abbot wanted the lot.

In the end, the town declared war on the monks and a huge mob stormed the abbey. They broke down the gates, beat the hell out of the screeching monks who tried to resist and generally looted and almost destroyed the interior.

The abbot was fortunately absent on a visit to London but when he returned, no doubt unaware and blissfully looking forward to a brief prayer and a hearty welcome, he was grabbed instead by the angry mob. They hauled him into the market place, shoved him down on his knees and presented him with a charter of liberties they were determined he would sign.

A chopping block and a headsman's axe stood ready if he refused. Of course he signed and, just as inevitably, he repudiated the document as soon as he was released.

The war continued. The monks armed themselves and attacked the townspeople in their own church, prompting the mob to storm the abbey again. For good measure they looted and burned all the abbey farms and abbey property they could reach. The Sherriff of Suffolk finally had to march in with a large force of soldiers and restore some sort of order. The leaders of the riots were all hanged and thirty cartloads of the rest were hauled off to Norwich Gaol. It took twenty years to repair the damage.

Hugh Despenser's father, also named Hugh, had been captured when Isabella's forces had besieged and stormed his castle at Bristol. The older Despenser was brutally hacked to pieces and the pieces were fed to the dogs.

Meanwhile Hugh Despenser the Younger was hanged, castrated and then drawn and quartered. Hanging, drawing and quartering was a common punishment for a king's enemies and traitors in those ghastly times, but the castration refinement was almost certainly a touch of queenly vengeance.

Edward's fate was more obscure. Legally he was still King of England and Isabella's husband, so he could not be publicly mutilated. Instead he was moved to a remote castle in Gloucestershire and later the news emerged that the king had died, supposedly from natural causes. The actual manner of his death has received much speculation. One of the many rumours was that he had been murdered with a red-hot poker. The murderers had used some kind of funnel to avoid any outer body burn scars and the poker had been thrust up the king's rectum. It was certainly a gruesome punishment that may well have been authorised by the She-Wolf of France.

AD 1328

THE LOST CITY UNDER THE SEA

BY HER VERY nature as an island, England has always been a maritime nation. Suffolk shoulders her way into the North Sea, giving some of the shortest lines of direct access to Europe and so Suffolk ports have always played a major role in defence and trade.

The old Roman port of Dunwich on the Suffolk coast had expanded by the twelfth century to become one of the largest ports in Britain. It is recorded as the seat of the first Bishop of East Anglia and received royal charters for both a mint and a market. It had a guildhall and the population was said to

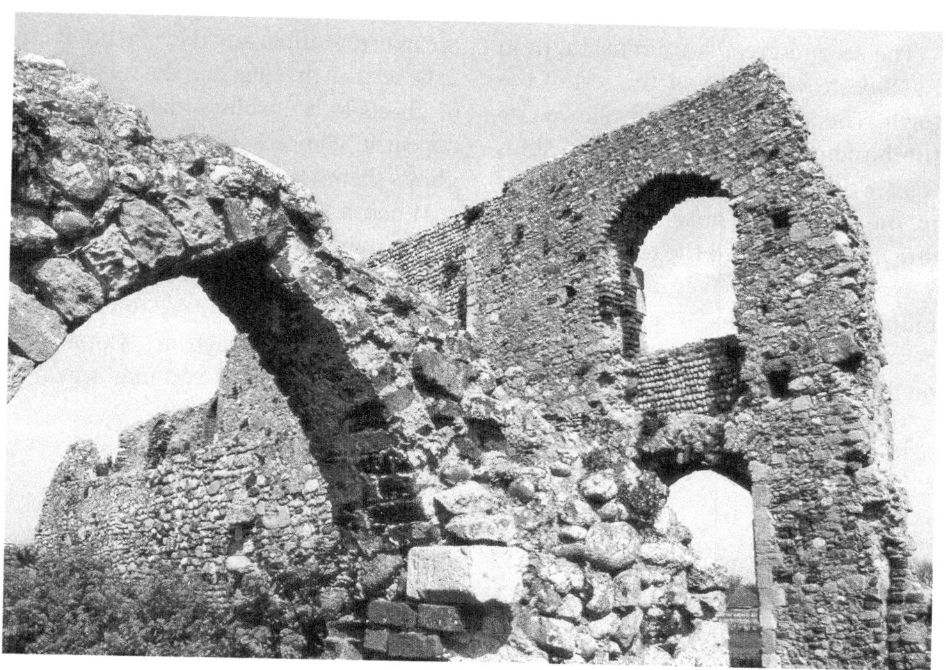

Dunwich Greyfriars Priory.

be around 5,000. It was a naval base as well as a major trading port, and from here Crusaders sailed on their perilous journeys to fight the Saracens in Palestine. It was also a religious centre with many fine churches and monasteries. Shipbuilding was a thriving industry and it was home to a large fishing fleet, which regularly ventured out to catch herring, and sailed to the cod-rich fishing grounds off Iceland.

It all came to an end with two terrible storms in 1287 and 1328, when the ferocious seas tore it all down and drowned the entire town. The savage North Sea was a cruel neighbour and over half the town's taxable farmland was lost to the pounding seas even before Domesday Book was written. A huge storm surge wiped out more of the low-lying portions of the town in the great gales of 1278.

The second great storm onslaught in 1328 destroyed much of the rest of the town. The advancing sea swallowed up the buildings it smashed down. Ships were wrecked and smashed to splinters in the harbour. Those who were not drowned abandoned the town and fled.

Now, only a fragment of one monastery remains. The ruins of the desolate Greyfriars Monastery still stands on the last cliff top, overlooking a shingle beach. All of the rest is under the waves. According to legend, when the sea is rough, the bells of the lost churches can be heard dolefully tolling beneath the grey heave of the rain-smashed waves.

Of course, serious historians get irked by this kind of tale, because there are no intact drowned churches under the sea. However, in recent years marine archaeologists have conducted an underwater survey to map out the offshore location of the lost city of Dunwich. Cameras have shown piles of stones and rubble on the seabed and divers have brought up sample blocks with medieval lime mortar still attached. The site is without doubt the remains of the largest underwater city in Europe.

So Dunwich is there. There are no intact churches with bells to be rung by the passing waves, just outlines and rubble. But everyone knows that ghosts are not substantial and they are not there to be seen all the time. It is the very nature of ghosts to be insubstantial and only to appear in glimpses. Ghost churches, like ghosts themselves, probably come and go.

When a storm rages in the black of night, when the winds howl and the waves crash and stir up the shingle on Dunwich beach, stand by the cliff top ruins of the old Greyfriars Monastery and who knows what you might hear ...

MORE LOST HARBOURS

The Saxon King Alfred is credited with the foundation of the English Navy when he ordered ships built to counter the predatory invasions of the Vikings. Dunwich, Blythburgh, Walberswick, Aldeburgh, Woodbridge and Ipswich were all great Suffolk shipbuilding ports. All of them built warships for a long succession of English kings, to guard against pirates or to take part in the seemingly endless wars against France, Spain and Holland.

All these ports were also great fishing ports and all rivals to Dunwich in their medieval heyday, but they too suffered inexorable decline in the later Middle Ages as the relentless North Sea and the shifting forces of sand and shingle conspired to seal off their estuaries.

In Aldeburgh the medieval Moot Hall was once a mile or more inland from the sea. Now it stands within a stone's throw of the advancing pebble beach. Blythburgh has virtually disappeared and all that is left is the magnificent flint church known as the Cathedral of the Marshes.

Aldeburgh, once a great shipbuilding port. The Old Moot Hall is only a pebble's throw away from the sea.

AD 1381

THE PEASANTS ARE REVOLTING

THE PEASANTS' REVOLT WAS a massive uprising of popular discontent aimed at breaking the iron hold of their overlords and masters. Most of all they wanted an end to their status as villein tenants or serfs. The main uprising began in Kent and quickly led to the storming of London, but all over East Anglia there were unanimous waves of sympathetic rebellion.

In Suffolk, the protests and the rioting were led by a man named John Wrawe. Even the parish priests had tired of the rapacious greed of the feudal landlords

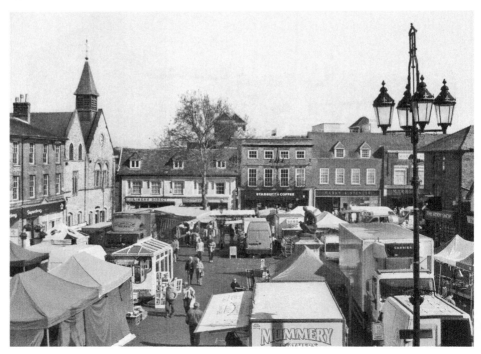

The Buttermarket at Bury St Edmunds. It is peaceful now, but it was once the scene of riots and beheadings.

THE PICKLED HEAD

Another Suffolk man who came to a grisly end in the dramatic days of the Peasants' Revolt was Simon Tybald of Sudbury. He had achieved the high ranks of Archbishop of Canterbury and Chancellor of England. In the first role he was hated for having excommunicated John Ball, a churchman who had been one of the main leaders of the revolt. In the second role he was even more loathed for having enforced the cruel Poll Tax.

St Gregory's church in Sudbury, where the pickled head is preserved. (Wikimedia)

When Wat Tyler's mob smashed their way into the Tower of London they captured Simon Tybald. With gleeful cheers and vicious curses, he was dragged out to Tower Hill and there beheaded in the crude and customary fashion. His skull was impaled for a while on a spike adorning Tower Bridge. Eventually it was taken down, pickled to preserve it and returned to Sudbury in Suffolk. This gruesome relic is still there, the empty eye sockets staring out from behind a glass panel in St Gregory's church.

and the pleasure-loving abbots in their great monasteries, and Wrawe was a dissident parson, possibly from Sudbury, although some sources claim he was from Ringsfield near Beccles. Another churchman named John Ball had angrily proclaimed that, 'We are all equal in Jesus Christ, yet the great lords treat us though we were only beasts of burden,' or words to that effect, and John Wrawe undoubtedly agreed with him.

Wrawe led the way in scouring the countryside, pillaging manor houses and burning court records. The rioters were attacking all landholders and trying to destroy the rolls that were the records of villein status. Flames and smoke stained the skies of Suffolk and soon Wrawe led his mob against the great abbey at Bury St Edmunds.

The townspeople of Bury were quick to welcome him, as their previous quarrels with the monks had left wounds that were still smarting. The abbey was attacked again by a huge mob. The monks had barricaded themselves inside, but with them were the Chief Justice and the local collector of taxes. The monks surrendered these two luckless individuals in the hope of saving themselves, but it was to no avail. The mob broke in and looted and burned the abbey yet again.

Somehow the Chief Justice, John de Lakenheath, seems to have dodged the rioters and fled back to his home village.

He was trying to escape even further, reaching for a boat on the river when it was kicked away from him by a local woman. He was grabbed and then hauled back to Bury, where he had his head chopped off in the market place, along with the tax collector.

The abbot had been warned that the mob was baying for his blood and had managed to run away before the rioters closed around the abbey. However, he only got as far as Mildenhall before he too was caught and beheaded like the rest.

Head-chopping had long been the chosen punishment of Parliament and kings. Now the common people were getting a taste for it too: cheers always went up when the heads rolled. The head of Bury's abbot was paraded triumphantly around the town.

Throughout Suffolk, the rebellion spread. Another group of rioters stormed Ipswich and burned down the offices of the archdeacon and the local tax officials. No landlord or government official was safe. They were all suddenly classified as 'Traitors to the People'.

The eruption was sudden and violent, but it did not last for long. King Richard II regained control of London, and Wat Tyler and the other rebel leaders there were all killed. The Bishop of Norwich rallied an army to crush the rebel forces in Norfolk. Approximately 600 royal soldiers marched into Suffolk and hanged large numbers of the rebels. By the end of the year, it was all over and nothing had been gained. The boy king Richard had initially agreed to some of the rebel claims but once his position was strong enough he rejected them all. 'Villeins you were and villeins you shall remain,' were his final words on the matter.

AD 1447

BEHEADED WITH A RUSTY SWORD

THE EARLDOM OF SUFFOLK was first created in 1336 for a wealthy landowner named Robert Ufford, who was an attendant at the court of King Edward III. By this time Edward had imprisoned his mother and executed her lover, so he was now King of England. The Uffords managed to lose the earldom after two generations and it was passed to another prominent family named de la Pole.

The de la Poles' fortunes were rather more mixed than the Uffords'. The first earl was hounded out of office, the second earl died during Henry V's expedition to France and the third earl got cut down at Agincourt. He was boiled up so that his flesh could be stripped away and only his bones were returned to England. Perhaps the sea passage was cheaper that way.

Enter the fourth earl of Suffolk, one William de la Pole. He was a political schemer who managed to become the most hated man in England. He played a major role in ensuring the ascension of the infant Henry VI. This was the period of the Hundred Years War and he pursued a strenuous military career, eventually becoming co-commander of the British forces at the Siege of Orléans. A young French girl named Joan of Arc defeated his attempts there and, in retreat, he was captured and spent three years as a prisoner in France. He eventually bounced back and became Lord High Admiral of England. He engineered the marriage of Henry VI to Margaret of Anjou and for that he was elevated to Marquess of Suffolk.

It seems that he had only one strong rival and opponent in the king's court and that was Humphrey, Duke of Gloucester. Humphrey was a Member of Parliament and the Privy Council and also an uncle and Lord Protector to the young king. He too had an honourable military career on the battlefields of France. He had contributed to the capture of Honfleur, fought at Agincourt and commanded the English garrison that had successfully repulsed the Siege of Calais. Unlike William, Humphrey was also popular with the people.

Humphrey should have been inviolate, but he made a fateful marriage that led to his downfall. His wife Eleanor was not liked and was accused of sorcery and heresy. William saw his chance and called for a meeting of Parliament to be convened at Bury St Edmunds. Suffolk was his stronghold and he knew he could pack the town with his own supporters.

When Duke Humphrey arrived, he was promptly arrested and charged with treason. He was confined in his lodgings at the St Saviour's hospital, not far from the great abbey. If Humphrey had come to trial, he might well have been acquitted and lived to wreak vengeance on his enemies. But this was not to be. The duke was found dead in his bed the next morning.

It was claimed as a natural death but the rumours soon surfaced that Duke Humphrey had been poisoned. King Henry and his queen were resident in Bury for this suspicious occasion and it was whispered that whatever devilry had taken place, it was probably with the connivance of the queen. Margaret of Anjou was also suspected of being William de la Pole's mistress.

Nothing was ever proved and with Humphrey dead, there was no real opposition. All of his lands and titles were up for grabs and William de la Pole got them all. A year later, he was elevated to the even grander title of Duke of Suffolk.

William was riding high and getting away with royal adultery and murder. He was greedy and drunk with power. Like most megalomaniacs, he probably thought he could get away with anything. It was even rumoured that he was planning to set his own son on the English throne.

But his contempt for the law, the throne and everyone around him had finally made him into the most hated man in England. Not only had he (supposedly) fornicated with the queen, usurped the power of the king and murdered a duke, he had also given away English lands in France. It was said that he had paid no monetary ransom

The ruined doorway to St Saviour's Hospital, where Sir Humphrey died.

THE BROWN MONK AND THE GREY LADY

Although William de la Pole and Queen Margaret were generally believed to be behind the murder of the Duke of Gloucester, there still remained the question of who had actually administered the fatal dose of poison. More speculation added to the gossip around Bury St Edmunds and one prime suspect eventually emerged.

She was a young nun named Maude Carew. She was in love with a monk at the abbey, who had been scheduled to appear as a witness at the duke's trial. If this had happened and the duke had subsequently been acquitted, then the monk would have been in dire danger of the duke's vengeance. This, it was whispered in the market place, was the story the evil queen had used to persuade the naive young nun to drip foul poison into the sleeping mouth of the tired old duke.

On dark nights do the ghostly apparitions of the Brown Monk and the Grey Lady glide through this empty doorway?

Maude had been duped into protecting her lover. To make the story juicier, secret tunnels connecting the Abbey and the old Fornham Road Priory to St Saviours had been her underground route of access.

Maude was spurned for her actions and took poison herself in remorse. Now, as the Brown Monk and the Grey Lady, they still haunt the abbey ruins in penance for their errors and sins.

for his release after his three years of captivity in France, and it was hinted that the price of his release might have included setting up Margaret's marriage to Henry and the return of her province of Anjou to the king of France.

By 1450 the wheel of fortune had turned and William's enemies were strong enough to bring him to trial; he was soon locked up in the Tower of London. The king intervened to save him from a death sentence (perhaps Queen Margaret was manipulating behind the scenes again) and William was banished from the realm for six years.

William almost escaped on a ship bound for Calais but now his enemies were riding high. His ship was intercepted by another and the Duke of Suffolk was forced to undergo a mock trial where the verdict was already decided. He was even denied the clean sharp axe of an experienced executioner. Instead, his head was hacked off by one of the sailors using a rusty sword. It took several clumsy and gruesome blows before the neck was severed. His body was thrown over the side and was eventually washed up on the beach at Dover.

AD 1514

THE DEFIANT BRIDE

Henry VII, the first of the Tudors. (THP)

SPEAK OF THE Tudors and immediately the flamboyant excesses of Henry VIII spring to mind, but the Tudor Age began at Bosworth Field, with Henry VII taking the Crown of England from Richard III. It was the culmination of the series of battles known as the Wars of the Roses, due to the red and white rose emblems of the rival houses of Lancaster and York, respectively.

Bosworth Field was in Leicestershire, but men from all over the country took part. Suffolk and Norfolk by this time were two of the richest counties in England, thanks to the buoyancy of the wool trade and their close links to the Continental markets. Their wealthy lords could afford to command large numbers of knights and men at arms.

The Duke of Norfolk commanded the vanguard of Richard's army and many men among his forces were recruited from his manors in Suffolk. At the end of the day he lay dead on the battlefield. Another Suffolk man, William Brandon of Henham, served on the Lancastrian side as the standard bearer to Henry. He too was slain, skewered by Richard's lance in the last great charge of the doomed king. The grateful Henry later took Brandon's son under his care and the youngster rose to become Sir Charles Brandon, Duke of Suffolk. The position became vacant when Henry VIII found cause to execute the last of the de la Poles.

The future Duke of Suffolk and Henry VIII, the next King of England, were consequently raised and educated together and became firm friends, a friendship that was to be tested later when Charles Brandon married Henry's sister Mary Tudor.

Mary had previously been married to Louis XII of France and when Louis died, Brandon was sent to congratulate the new French king, Francis I, and to negotiate Mary's safe return to England. Marriages among nobility and royalty were very much political and financial affairs, and in this case there was also the return of Mary's substantial dowry of gold plate and jewels to be resolved.

Henry already had plans to marry his sister off again. He still wanted an alliance with France and had another

CARDINAL WOLSEY

The eminent churchman Cardinal Thomas Wolsey was also a son of Suffolk. Until his downfall in 1530, when Wolsey died a broken man on his way to be tried for treason, Brandon and Wolsey together were the two dominant figures in the king's court and counsels.

Wolsey was born in Ipswich, probably the son of a butcher, and rose to become Henry VIII's First Minister, his High Chancellor and Chief Councillor. Wolsey was Henry's negotiator with the Pope and through Wolsey, Henry controlled the clergy. For fourteen years Wolsey was at the top of the political tree. He planned a magnificent college in his hometown of Ipswich, which was never completed. The striking red brick arch of its gateway close to St Peter's church is all that now remains of this cherished dream.

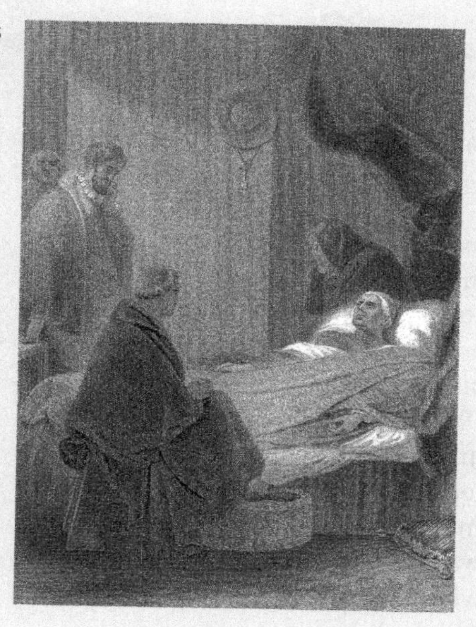

The death of Cardinal Wolsey. (THP)

Wolsey's greatest achievement was to organise the peace conference between Henry and Francis I of France on the Field of the Cloth of Gold. However, even his superb negotiating skills failed to bend the Pope to Henry's will over the vexed question of the monarch's continuing parade of divorced or executed wives. In the end Wolsey's failure to get what Henry wanted led to his arrest and would probably have cost him his head if he had lived long enough to come to trial.

The death charge of Richard III at Bosworth Field: he killed Brandon before he was brought to the ground. (THP)

member of the French royal house in mind. However, Mary Tudor was a head-strong young woman with ideas and passions of her own. She had married once for England and once was enough. Old King Louis had, fortunately, died quickly. The marriage had only lasted for eighty-two days. Now she wanted to marry to please herself and her choice was her childhood sweetheart: the man who had been sent to fetch her home, Charles Brandon.

The couple pulled a fast one; instead of returning home, they stayed in France and married there. They waited in France, no doubt sweating a bit, wondering if Henry would have them punished or remember their happy play days together. Would he play the outraged king or the tolerant friend and brother?

It was a love story that almost cost the impetuous couple their heads and did cost them a fortune in financial settlement. However, for once the story did not end in spurting blood and rolling heads. Henry had not yet fully developed his taste for head-chopping. He forgave them but he did hit them with a hefty fine to recompense for the loss to his treasury.

AD 1553

BLOODY MARY

BLOODY MARY WAS Queen of England from 1553 to 1558: she was a very tough lady and, despite her short rule, one of the most hated rulers in our country's history.

When Henry VIII died in 1547, he left three children, Mary, Elizabeth and Edward. The 9-year-old Edward became Edward VI. However, the boy proved a sickly king, who died six years later of tuberculosis. Edward was a passionate Protestant and he hated his oldest sister, Mary, who was staunchly Catholic. Henry VIII had made a will in which Edward, Mary, and his second daughter Elizabeth were all to succeed him in turn if this became necessary. Edward saw that Mary could become Queen of England and attempted to stop this with a will of his own.

The Duke of Cumberland had been nominated as Edward's protector. Cumberland saw that his own grip on power would vanish if Edward was replaced by Mary, so he persuaded Edward to name his son's wife, Lady Jane Grey, as the next queen. Lady Jane was a granddaughter of Henry VII, and the daughter of the Mary Tudor who married Charles Brandon in the last chapter, so there was a tenuous link to the royal line.

The whole business almost spilled into civil war and in the event, Queen Jane only reigned for nine days. Edward had tried to claim that his sisters Mary and Elizabeth were illegitimate, but Mary was having none of that. She was the legitimate daughter of Henry VIII and his first wife Catherine of Aragon, and so had the true right of succession.

Mary was summoned to London to pay her last respects to her dying brother. However, she was later warned that this was just a pretext to capture and detain her while Jane Grey was declared queen. Mary managed to escape from London and fled to her castle at Framlingham. She knew that most of East Anglia would support her. Jane and her husband, Lord Guildford Dudley, had no friends here. After all, his father was John Dudley, Earl of Northumberland – the man who had recently undertaken the task of crushing the Kett Rebellion in the Eastern counties.

Mary raised her standard at Framlingham Castle and rallied her own followers. With most of the Suffolk and Norfolk gentry behind her she marched on London, displaced Lady Jane and had her condemned to death. Lady Jane and her husband were both executed: they went to the block and faced the headsman's axe. Mary had obviously learned a trick or two from watching her father.

Mary Tudor was now Queen of England, and she was a very bitter woman with a lot of other axes to grind. She had been separated from her mother and rejected and declared a bastard by her father. Her brother had scorned her. Her mother's religion, to which she too adhered, had been crushed and brutally suppressed. Hell hath no fury like a woman with plentiful grievances and Mary had more than enough. Now it was time for revenge and to turn the nature of religious faith back to its natural course.

Mary set about overturning the rise of Protestantism and restoring Catholicism. She was determined to reunite the English Church with Rome, and she began by cancelling all the religious laws favouring Protestantism that her father and her brother had established, and then married her cousin Philip, who was the heir to the throne of Spain. Philip became the joint ruler of England and England was now in alliance with one of the major Catholic powers of Europe.

Of course, all of this reversal was not done without opposition. Mary made herself very unpopular and inevitably there was Protestant opposition. Mary's reaction was brutal, and during her reign at least 280 Protestant martyrs were burned to death. Mary had reinstated the medieval laws against heresy, which brought with them the

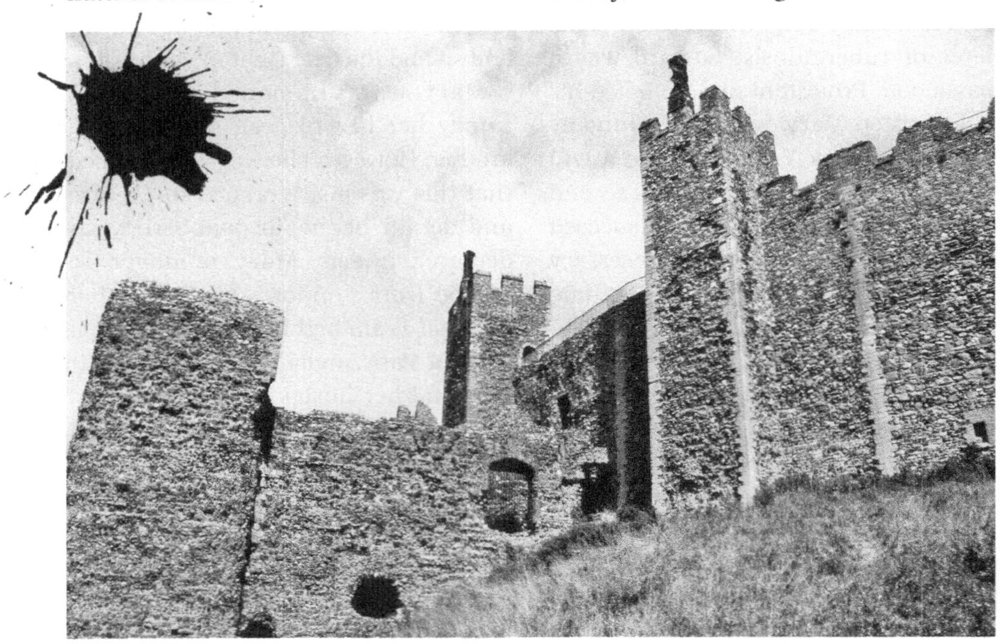

Framlingham Castle, where Mary raised her banners.

death penalty for those who would not conform to the practises of the Roman Catholic faith. Those who were found guilty of such heresy were tied to stakes and surrounded by piles of brushwood, which were then set on fire.

One of the first churchmen to be burned, and the first to be burned in Suffolk, was Rowland Taylor, the rector of Hadleigh. Taylor had incurred Mary's wrath by supporting Lady Jane Grey during her fleeting accession to the throne. Most of the East Anglian gentlemen who had marched with Mary had probably not been prepared for her vicious return to Catholicism. Taylor perhaps had been less naïve.

Taylor was arrested, imprisoned and sentenced to death. The sentence was carried out at his own rectory at Hadleigh, on Aldham Common just outside the town. Hundreds more deaths were to follow. The first executions were all of senior churchmen, but then the whole business got out of hand. Those burned in Bury St Edmunds included a sawyer, a labourer, a wheelwright, a husbandman, two weavers and a servant of the crown. The range of victims was wide and filtered down through all classes.

They were all executed on Thingoe Hill, a small hill just outside Bury St Edmunds, which was the normal gathering place for the spectacle of burnings and hangings. Today there is a small white monument on Aldham Common that marks the spot where Rowland Taylor was burned to death. It is fenced in by neat black iron railings. In a peaceful corner of the old churchyard, facing the green and the cathedral in the abbey gardens at Bury St Edmunds, there is another memorial to the Protestant martyrs who were burned in the town.

Guarding the gate at Framlingham Castle.

Their courage and commitment to their faith is commemorated, but nowhere is there any memorial to Queen Mary Tudor. Her five-year reign brought nothing but repression, rebellions and resentment. Her alliance with Spain led to a joint war with France and the loss of Calais, which was the last English possession on French soil. Her marriage with Philip failed. She is said to have died of a broken heart, unmourned, and she became generally known as Bloody Mary, or one of the most evil women in history.

AD 1586

SUFFOLK'S BUCCANEER

HENRY VIII HAD ORDERED the building of a new wave of ships after his break with Rome, knowing that he had made serious enemies of Catholic France and Spain and predicting the threat of the Spanish Armada. Drake's ship was one of the last great galleons to be built in Aldeburgh.

In 1540, Queen Elizabeth I commissioned Francis Drake to make the first circumnavigation of the globe. Drake set off with a fleet of five ships, including his flagship, the *Pelican*, as she had been named by her Suffolk builders. They sailed south-west through the Atlantic, rounding the ferocious Cape Horn with its mountainous seas. The voyage continued north into the Pacific to the coast of California, west again through the Philippines and around the Cape of Good Hope.

Felixstowe beach, near to where Cavendish was born. (LC-DIG-ppmsc-08373)

Two years had passed before the gallant *Pelican* re-entered Plymouth Sound, and she was alone. Drake had lost four of his five ships, but the sturdy Suffolk vessel had endured. Drake brought back a navigational triumph and a fortune in Spanish treasure that he had looted on the way. He was knighted by the grateful queen on the deck of his ship, which had by then been renamed as the *Golden Hind*.

Drake's success was only the beginning. The Elizabethan Age saw the magnificent rise of England's maritime power, with voyages of exploration to every corner of the globe. It was an age of expansion, heroism on the high seas and wars with Spain; a time for pirates and adventurers, foremost among which was Suffolk's own Sir Thomas Cavendish. Cavendish was born in 1560 in the small village of Trimley St Martin, close to modern-day Felixstowe and within sight of the sea.

The young Queen Elizabeth had ascended to the throne only two years before, so the boy Thomas grew up into that blossoming age of big sailed ships and exotic new horizons. His father was a wealthy man who left him a fortune. He attended Corpus Christi College in Cambridge but left university without taking his degree.

He earned his title, 'The Navigator', by making the first planned circumnavigation of the globe. Drake and a few others had sailed around the world before him, but their voyages had been mostly by chance, with no defined intention of what they eventually accomplished before they had sailed from their home ports. Cavendish, in contrast, did plot his course and navigate his way around the oceans.

He spent a few years in luxurious living and dabbled briefly in politics, becoming MP for Shaftesbury in Dorset. But the sea was in his blood and he wanted the salt wind in his hair. In 1585 he sailed with Sir Richard Grenville on a voyage to Virginia, crossing the Atlantic to take settlers to the new American colonies.

A year later Spain and England were at war and Cavendish was determined to follow the privateer example of Sir Francis Drake who was attacking and plundering Spanish treasure ships in the Pacific. Cavendish used his fortune to build his own ship, a sailing vessel of 120 tons, which he named the *Desire*. With two smaller ships – the 60-ton *Content* and the 40-ton *Hugh Gallant* – he too set sail as a licensed privateer.

With three ships and 122 men, Cavendish sailed from Plymouth in July of 1586 and reached Cape Horn and the Strait of Magellan in January of 1587, nearly six months later. Navigation in those days was mainly by use of an astrolabe, through which Cavendish could calculate his longitude by measuring the sun's angle above the horizon.

Landing on an island off present-day Punta Arenas in Chile, Cavendish's sailors killed and salted barrels of penguins to augment their food supply and then the three ships sailed into the Pacific and turned up the western coast of South America. Now the bloody business of the expedition really began. The small English fleet sighted and then sank or captured up to nine Spanish ships, as well as raiding a number of small towns for supplies and treasure. It was not without cost. The butcher's bill was heavy and soon Cavendish no longer had enough men to man all three of his ships. He had to abandon and sink the *Hugh Gallant* and use the survivors of her crew to supplement the crews of *Desire* and *Content*.

From the pilot of one of the captured Spanish ships, Cavendish learned that a Spanish treasure galleon was expected to arrive at Cape St Lucas on the Baja California peninsula. Immediately he hoisted all sails and raced north to intercept the prize. When the *Santa Anna* was sighted she proved to be a galleon of 600 tons, much larger than Cavendish's two smaller ships put together. But the Spaniard's decks had been cleared of cannon to make more room for her precious cargo, and that left her at the mercy of the hungry privateers' two ships.

Cavendish raked the Spaniards' decks with cannonballs and grapeshot as she fled across the sea. The bigger ship could not outrun the English predators and as her sails were tumbled, her captain finally struck his colours and surrendered. Her holds were filled with silver, spices, silks and gold and Cavendish could only pick out the best of this rich haul as his own small ships could not hold it

THE FIRST PILGRIMS

Suffolk's major ports of the early Middle Ages may have been eroded by the ravages of the cruel North Sea, but a new port was booming. Now Ipswich had become home to forests of mast and rigging as the harbour (and consequently, trade) expanded, and Suffolk men had major roles to play in this brave new world.

Model of the Mayflower. *(LC-USZ62-3135)*

Columbus had discovered America, but this huge new land still had to be tamed and settled. Much of this was dreamed and planned behind the moat and walls of beautiful Otley Hall, just 7 miles north of Ipswich. It was the home of the Suffolk mariner Bartholomew Gosnold, who financed and led two voyages to the New World. In 1602 he discovered and named Cape Cod and Martha's Vineyard. In 1607 he returned to found the Jamestown Colony, the first English-speaking settlement in America.

This was sixteen years before the Pilgrim Fathers sailed in the *Mayflower*, which was built just across the Orwell/Stour estuary in Harwich.

Ipswich continued as Suffolk's premier port and a major centre for voyages carrying emigrants to New England.

all. The surviving Spanish sailors were set ashore and the *Santa Anna* set on fire. Leaving the blazing galleon behind them, Cavendish headed his ships out into the Pacific on the long journey home.

The weather separated them and the *Content* was lost somewhere in the blue vastness of the Pacific, never to be seen again. The *Desire* finally reached the island of Guam in January of 1588. Cavendish made more landfalls in the Philippines and Java to trade for food and supplies and then sailed across the Indian Ocean to the coast of Africa. He rounded the Cape of Good Hope and then made the long haul up through the Atlantic to arrive back in Plymouth in September that year. The entire circumnavigation of the globe had taken two years and forty-nine days, and Thomas Cavendish was still only 28 years old.

He was knighted by Queen Elizabeth and three years later set sail on his second and last expedition. He lost most of his crew in a battle with the Portuguese off the coast of Brazil and headed back across the Atlantic towards Saint Helena, but died at sea somewhere in the South Atlantic.

His exploits have been somewhat overshadowed by those of Sir Francis Drake and Sir Walter Raleigh. Those two piratical Elizabethan adventurers have tended to hog the pages of the history books. But Sir Thomas Cavendish was an equally flamboyant hero of the age; just as courageous, just as successful, and playing a part for Suffolk in opening up the sea routes of the widening world.

AD 1605

GUNPOWDER, TREASON AND PLOT

THE STUART AGE WAS a traumatic time for England as a nation. It was a time of civil war between king and Parliament and of violent shifts in faith from Catholicism to the new Protestant Anglican church. Henry VIII had broken the links with Rome; Queen Mary, in her short reign, had tried to restore them. Queen Elizabeth had switched the nation partially back on the Anglican track; James I, the first Stuart king, was another Protestant. It all ended in two rounds of civil war, the beheading of King Charles I and, eventually, the restoration of the monarchy with King Charles II.

The Houses of Parliament, the target for the Gunpowder Plot. (LC-DIG-PPMSC-08560)

James I, who was already James VI of Scotland, arrived in London from Edinburgh in April of 1603. At first he had a rapturous reception but things soon turned sour and in 1605 a group of Catholics decided that the new king, his son and his Parliament all had to go.

The Gunpowder Plotters aimed to fill one of the cellars below the Houses of Parliament with barrels of gunpowder and blow up the building and all those within it.

Guy Fawkes has become the figure most associated with the plot, but in reality he was only the mercenary hired to place the powder barrels. The leader of the plot was Robert Catesby, a Northamptonshire gentleman, and one of the chief financiers was Ambrose Rookwood of Staningfield in Suffolk. Rookwood not only supplied much of the money for powder and weapons, but he also had a fine stable to provide transport and communications.

The plot failed when one of the conspirators sent a warning note to one of the Catholic ministers due to attend the planned opening ceremony of Parliament. It was apparently deemed not sinful to kill the king and his Protestant ministers, but Parliament was still a mixed bag. The letter was passed to the king, the cellars were promptly searched and Guy Fawkes was discovered with the powder barrels.

The rest of the plotters fled. Rookwood was the last to leave London, but he escaped using a relay of his best horses. They were all eventually captured and Rookwood was hanged at Westminster Yard alongside Fawkes and two other conspirators.

At the scaffold, the Suffolk man made a speech that brought many in the crowd to tears. He confessed to his crime but prayed for God to bless the king and turn him into a Catholic.

The Gunpowder Conspirators. From left to right: Bates, Robert Winter, Christopher and John Wright, Thomas Percy, Guy Fawkes, Robert Catesby and Thomas Winter. (THP)

AD 1642

THE CIVIL WAR

CHARLES I WAS DEVOTED to the Church of England but he also believed in the ancient God-given right of a king to rule his kingdom, which did not sit well with his fledgling Parliament. It was a conflict that brought him into head-on opposition with Oliver Cromwell and was soon to escalate into a vicious civil war.

Suffolk was not the scene of any of the major battles between the flamboyant Cavaliers and the puritanical Roundheads, but neither did the county escape entirely from the nationwide turmoil. East Anglia generally was a Parliamentarian stronghold: Oliver Cromwell, who became Lord Protector of the Commonwealth of England, Scotland and Ireland after the execution of the

'A PLAIN AND RUSSET COATED CAPTAIN'

Most of the ordinary folk of Suffolk were firmly behind the Roundheads and Cromwell's dream of a new parliamentary order. They were kept down by taxes, prices and suppressed wages, and sick to death of the old hierarchy of king, barons and abbots who generally exploited them without mercy. Quite a few middle-ranking gentleman and yeoman farmers joined them and one of these was Ralph Margery from Walsham le Willows.

Ralph was a solid Puritan who volunteered to fight against the despised king. He collected horses and men and raised his own troop of cavalry, which became the 13th troop of Cromwell's Ironsides. It was this doughty Suffolk man that Cromwell praised when he said he would, 'rather have a plain and russet-coated captain that knows what he fights for, and loves what he knows, than that which you call a gentleman ...'

Through the roar of cannonballs and hails of musket shot Margery led his troop into battle at Naseby, which was the decisive battle of the Civil War. The Royalist forces were shattered by the charges of the Ironsides and the king lost all his veteran infantry and all his artillery. After Naseby there were only mopping-up operations and the sordid and long drawn-out business of the trial and executing the king.

king, was the Member of Parliament for Cambridge and drew much of his New Model Army from this region. However, many of the gentry were still Catholics and Royalist supporters.

There were various riots and upheavals across the two counties as Protestant mobs attacked Catholic homes. In Lowestoft, the Royalist gentry took control but Cromwell himself rode to confront them with 1,000 horsemen and quickly put down their rebellion.

One Suffolk family of Royalist gentry that secretly supported the king was the Tollemache family of Helmingham Hall. This lovely old moated manor house was built between 1480 and 1510, and many of its high brick chimneys are partially original. Today it is a splendid picture of rich red brick walls and gables, with wide white windows and doors, all reflected back in the serene waters of the 60ft-wide encircling moat.

The two drawbridges that span the moat have been pulled up every night since the time of the Civil War. It is a precaution that began when the house was the headquarters of a Royalist secret society called The Sealed Knot. Charles I had been executed but his son, Charles Stuart, was in exile in France. The New Parliament proved to be as inept and unpopular as the old king and there were soon calls for the restoration of the monarch. The Sealed Knot, dedicated to this purpose, was formed during the Protectorate of Oliver Cromwell and, after much plotting and eight attempts, they were eventually successful in restoring King Charles II to his throne.

Helmingham Hall was once the Suffolk centre of the Sealed Knot Society. (THP)

AD 1665

THE ROAR OF CANNON AND THE STINK OF BLOOD

SIR FRANCIS DRAKE had smashed the Spanish Armada in 1588, but there was one more foe to be beaten before Britannia could be said to rule the waves.

England's other maritime rival in this age of growing sea power was Holland. The Dutch were carving their empire in the East Indies, comfortably out of the way of most of Britain's empire building, but at home they contested the mastery of the North Sea. They came into conflict with Britain over trade and fishing rights and the battles that decided these issues were fought off the coast of Suffolk, in sight and sound of the Suffolk shore.

The first great battle was fought off the town of Lowestoft in 1665.

The harbour at Lowestoft. (LC-DIG-PPMSC-08612)

The two fleets each numbered more than 100 ships. The English fleet was commanded by James Stuart, the Duke of York, in the *Royal Charles*. It was an armada of more than 4,500 guns and more than 22,000 men. The Dutch fleet had a few less ships – 103 to fight England's 109 – with 21,000 men, but 4,800 guns, so the two sides were fairly evenly matched.

The English fleet had already successfully blockaded the Dutch ports, but had been forced to withdraw to resupply. The Dutch feared that they were about to be blockaded again and sailed out to meet them, commanded by Lieutenant Admiral Van Wassenaer in a ship named the *De Eandracht*.

There does not seem to be a fully coherent account of the battle, which was a confused and bloody affair. Like all sea battles, the key was to gain the best position with the advantage of the prevailing winds. Perhaps the breeze didn't play fair and changed direction a few times. The two fleets jostled for position, passing each other a couple of times on the opposite tack, and by the time they did engage, the Dutch had lost their battle line formation.

It was a long hot day and throughout the thunder of cannon roared and the smoke and fire stained the cloudless blue of the sky. The sounds of battle carried clearly to the Suffolk farmers working in their fields 40 miles away. The smoke columns were plain to see, although the ships were below the horizon, and the scent of cordite and the stink of blood were wafted on the winds.

The Dutch had gained the leeward position, which should have given them the advantage of a superior range for their guns, but their squadrons had blocked each other and their chain of command had broken. Many of

Dutch warships of the era (With kind permission of the Thomas Rare Book Library, University of Toronto).

their ships were not naval vessels but merchant ships rigged for war, and their captains possessed an independence of mind that did not quite make up for their lack of squadron discipline.

The English sailed into them and bloody slaughter ensued. Sails and rigging were torn by grapeshot on both sides. Cannon broadsides swept the decks at close quarters, killing and maiming in bloody fury. Sails and masts crashed down and burst into flames. The battle lasted from dawn till dusk and fire and death was the grand order of the day.

The Dutch had the misfortune to lose two of their squadron commanders in quick succession. One lieutenant admiral had his hip smashed away by a cannonball, while the other was hit squarely in the stomach and literally torn in two. Van Wassenaer in the *De Eandracht* didn't even know that he had lost his two key flag officers. Like gladiators of old, Duke James in the *Royal Charles* had closed with the *De Eandracht* and the two flagships were fighting a broadside-to-broadside duel. They pounded each other until a shot from the *Royal James* found the powder magazine of the *De Eandracht*. The Dutch ship exploded with a mighty roar of erupting flame that shook every other battling ship on the red-stained ocean.

The fickle wind had changed, blowing the first two English squadrons even further into the confused mass of Dutch ships but allowing the third rearguard English squadron to sweep round and cut off the Dutch retreat. The Dutch fleet was now trapped and virtually at the mercy of the British cannon. With Van Wassenaer dead, the Dutch were leaderless and, having seen the *De Eanderacht* blown apart, many of the Dutch captains lost heart and faltered. Their English counterparts sensed victory and pressed their advantage ruthlessly.

By the end of the day, half of the survivors of the Dutch fleet were running for the safety of a home port. Seventeen Dutch ships were lost and over 2,000 Dutch sailors were killed. The English fleet lost one ship and between 300 and 500 men were killed. Over 2,000 Dutch prisoners were taken or rescued from the sea and landed the next morning at Lowestoft and Southwold, along with hundreds of wounded. The Dutch fleet had been routed but the stakes were high and five years later they would be back off the coast of Suffolk for yet another great sea battle.

AD 1667

THE LAST INVASION

THE ANGLO-DUTCH WARS WERE mainly fought at sea by means of pitched fleet-size sea battles and attempts by both fleets to blockade the ports of the other. At the same time there was the constant fear of a Dutch invasion along the Suffolk coast, and so militias and fortifications were kept on alert. The scares and rumours came and went, and then suddenly the invasion happened.

The Dutch had established a blockade of the Thames estuary, but could not penetrate any further into London's river. So they decided to attack the port of Harwich on the Essex side of the Stour and Orwell estuary. Harwich was the major naval port on the East Anglian coast, protected by its own fort and a thin line of warships across the port entrance, as well as Landguard Fort, on the opposite side of the estuary.

The key to taking Harwich was to first take Landguard Fort on the Suffolk side of the double river mouth. This is what the Dutch attempted to do.

Dutch longboats from the Dutch ships offshore landed a force of 1,500 marines and 500 sailors on the beach at Felixstowe. They were commanded by an English colonel named Thomas Dolman, one of many of Cromwell's bitter, diehard soldiers who had turned traitor after Charles II was returned to the throne. They had landed at Cobbold's Point, which was north of the fort and out of range of its guns. It enabled them to make a safe landing but also meant that they now had to march south along the beach and drag their cannon with them across the shingle before they could commence their attack.

Dolman split his forces, taking his marines along the beach and leaving the sailors to protect their rear and the boats. Soon the sailors came under fire from the local Suffolk militia, organised and commanded by the Earl of Suffolk, who showered them with musket fire from the cliff tops. After struggling across the shingle, Dolman marshalled his troops and launched his attack on the fort, opening up with small cannon fire and trying to rush the walls with scaling ladders.

Landguard Fort was commanded by Captain Nathanial Darell. His garrison numbered approximately 100 officers and men to man forty cannons. They would not have been enough against Dolman's superior force of marines but fortune favoured the defence. The fort, and Felixstowe, were providing R&R for 400 veteran musketeers, who were resting after two and a half years of continuous fighting against the Dutch.

The Dutch attacked with cannon fire, muskets, pikes, cutlasses and grenades. Darell's cannons returned fire and the British musketeers made their presence felt. They were well practised and experienced. They flitted from one gun port to the next, never appearing twice in succession from the same firing position. Each shot they fired was well aimed and precise. They worked as pairs and as they moved, the marksman would exchange his empty musket for a primed and loaded musket from the man behind.

The noise was horrendous – the boom of the cannons, the bang of muskets, the explosions of grenades and the shrieks and screams of those who were hit by the flying missiles. But there was very little shouting: both sides knew their job and worked with a minimum of urging or ordering. The British grenadiers paced the inside of the thick stone walls, listening for the thud of a scaling ladder. As the first

LANDGUARD FORT

This massive red-brick pentagon stands on a site that is steeped in Suffolk history. For centuries, traders and raiders have sailed past this point, to enter or depart from a double-pronged estuary into the heart of Suffolk. Viking longboats, tall-mast schooners, warships and Thames barges, as well as the sleek modern yachts that fill these waters today, all have flaunted their sails here in the fresh Suffolk breeze.

With the great trading nations of Europe always in competition verging on piracy and warfare, there has always been a threat, and so there have been many different fortifications built on this site. Henry VIII had two blockhouses built here in 1543. In 1628, a new square wood fort was built with a bastion on each corner, which was surrounded by the first brick wall on the order of Charles II.

The Dutch attempt to storm the walls in 1667 was the fort's finest hour. The fort was reconstructed twice through the eighteenth century, leaving us the huge outer walls we see today.

As cannon and muskets became obsolete, so the fort in its original role became redundant. It was used mainly as a barracks, although during the Second World War it housed mobile and fixed anti-aircraft guns, which were used against German bombers. Today, after extensive repairs to make the monument safe, it has become an acknowledged heritage site and a museum.

Dutchman tried to climb over the wall, the grenadier would duck under the swing of his cutlass and neatly drop a grenade over the wall. As the grenade exploded it would blast the ladder away.

The Dutch were beaten back, but they regrouped and came back for a second ferocious attack. Despite the blockade one small British ship, a galliot with a crew of about twenty-five men, was close enough to hit the beach with grapeshot. As the shots hit the beach, they turned the layer of heavy pebbles into shrapnel, which smashed into the Dutch troops.

Still the Dutch came in blue-uniformed waves. Dolman brandished a sword above his head, waving it in a cutting stroke to signal his men to advance. A sharp-eyed English musketeer spotted him and picked him out as the troop commander. Dolman had invited his own death and immediately it was granted. One shot was fired from the English musket and Dolman fell. Captain Darell leaned out from a firing position to see what had happened and he too took a musket ball in the shoulder. However, he was still able to continue commanding the battle.

The bluecoats were now staggering in their advance. They reached the wall again with their scaling ladders but without Dolman to command them, they faltered. The Dutch soon began to retreat and Darell gave the order to cease firing. The invaders retreated to their landing point but were trapped there by low water. They had to wait for the tide to turn before they could launch their boats and return to their ships.

The Dutch had lost 150 men, either killed, wounded or captured. The English casualties were only ten.

AD 1672

CAUGHT WITH THEIR PANTS DOWN

THE ANGLO-DUTCH WARS CONTINUED for a third round of bloody naval battles as England and Holland wrestled for control of the North Sea. In May 1672, a Dutch squadron of frigates sailed down the English Channel in the hope of repeating a previous attack on the Medway.

Southwold, the signal mast and the lighthouse.

This time they found the fort at Sheerness well prepared and ready for them and their commander decided on discretion as the better part of valour. He returned with his ships up the channel and ran into a huge stroke of luck.

A combined British and French fleet under the command of the Duke of York and the Earl of Sandwich had put into Sole Bay off Southwold for repairs and careening. The ships were caught at anchor with their sails furled, and many of the British sailors were literally caught with their pants down, having spent the night doing what sailors usually do whenever they are allowed ashore.

As the enemy's wind-filled sails hove over the horizon, the alarms sounded and the moored ships burst into frenzied activity as officers bellowed and men ran to haul up anchors and lower the sails. Those ashore tumbled out of the alehouses and raced through the streets to the harbour and the shore boats, blinking through their hangovers and struggling to pull on their clothes. No doubt they were followed by a few wails and curses from any of their lady friends who had not been shrewd enough to demand payment in advance for their services.

In desperate haste the fleet weighed anchor and tried to manoeuvre for some sea room as the Dutch closed in and the Dutch guns opened fire. The Dutch fleet numbered 75 ships with nearly 5,000 guns. The combined British and French fleets totalled 93 ships with just over 6,000 guns, but they were caught with flapping sails and trapped against the lee shore. The French contingent tried to avoid the battle but the British ships were soon at close quarters.

It was another dawn to dusk battle, but this time the fighting ships were so close to shore that those who lined the Southwold cliffs had a grandstand view of the action. They watched with horror as the great mass of ships collided with a thunder of cannon. Flames and smoke gushed into the sky and the screams of dying and wounded men were mixed in with the nightmare noise of the battle.

The British fleet had been caught unawares, but they responded magnificently. Despite their initial disadvantage of having to tack against the wind, British seamanship and British courage began to tilt the balance, although at one stage the outcome was so uncertain that the male observers on the cliffs were told to stand by and prepare for a Dutch invasion.

The Dutch had singled out the two British flagships: the *Prince*, carrying the Duke of York, and the *Royal James*, carrying Admiral Edward Montague, the Earl of Sandwich. With merciless bombardment they encircled and tried to sink the two prizes.

The captain of the Dutch ship *Groot Hollandia* succeeded in getting grapnel lines aboard the *Royal James* and battered her hull as their sailors fought with swords and muskets. Finally more English sloops got their boarding lines on to the *Groot Hollandia*, and English boarding parties stormed on to the Dutch ship. The Dutch captain was forced to cut his lines to the *Royal James* and back off to clear his own decks of the enemy.

The *Royal James* drifted away, already sinking, her masts broken and half of her company dead or dying. The Dutch attacked her with fireboats. Two were sunk but the third collided with the British warship. The *Royal James* was soon burning fiercely. The flames reached her powder magazine and now it was the turn of a British flagship to explode with a devastating roar of sound and fire.

The battle continued until daylight faded. The wind shifted and this time in the British fleet's favour, but still the battle was deemed inconclusive: both sides claimed a victory. The Duke of York survived, having changed his flagship twice. Edward Montague, however, was fished out of the sea two weeks later. His body was only recognisable by the George and Star of Garter ribbon still hanging on his breast.

AD 1683

A MURDER PLOT THAT FAILED

IT WAS IN the seventeenth century that King James I discovered the equestrian pleasures of Newmarket, first to indulge in his passion for hare hunting on the heath, and then to enjoy the racing. The first recorded race was run in 1622. It was a two-horse race between horses belonging to Lord Salisbury and the Marquis of Buckingham. The wager was for £30, an enormous sum at the time. Buckingham's horse won and it was the beginning of the entire history of thundering hooves, screaming excitement and the joy or despair of fortunes being lost or won.

Charles I and his son Charles II, famously known as 'The Merry Monarch', continued the royal passion for the sporting pleasures of the turf. Charles II was a keen rider who moved his court to Newmarket every summer for the racing season. He built Palace House as his second home and for a while Newmarket was even known as the unofficial second capital of England.

The first race ever to be run under written rules was the Town Plate Race, which first took place in 1666. Charles had created the race by a decree in Parliament the previous year and rode his own horse to victory in the race of 1671. The race is still run at Newmarket every year and is the oldest surviving official horse race.

Horse racing has been the sport of kings and queens ever since. At one stage, during the English Civil War, Newmarket was suspected of being a cover for Royalist sympathies and disaffection. It was a fair enough assumption, but with most of Cambridgeshire solidly behind Cromwell and his Roundheads, the Royalists at Newmarket were probably wise to keep quiet and to keep their heads down.

In 1683 the king returned to Newmarket with his brother James, the Duke of York, both of them planning to enjoy more of the sport that thrilled their royal blood. Charles was looking forward to a few days of racing and gambling, and perhaps a few hours of amorous dalliance with Nell Gwynne.

Perhaps he did get in a few hours of sport with Nell, but the racing was not to be. The Great Fire of Newmarket swept through the town and sixty homes in the High Street were engulfed in the flames. The king and his friends fled from the burning town, no doubt cursing the fact that their planned entertainment had been cancelled. Charles did not know it until later, but the tragedy of Newmarket had saved his life.

An assassination attempt had been carefully planned. The plotters had intended to take over Rye House in Hertfordshire, which lay beside the king's route on his way home to London. The house was leased by a Civil War veteran who had fought on the Parliamentarian side. The grounds of the house gave good cover for an ambush and Charles would have been shot down and killed in a swift, sudden attack with pistols and muskets.

The terrifying blaze at Newmarket had forced the king and his party to return home earlier than expected. The change of schedule meant that the ambush party had no time to get into position, so the plot failed and was subsequently discovered. Eleven conspirators, including two Members of Parliament, were tried and sentenced to death for the crime of treason. Two were hanged, six were hanged, drawn and quartered, two were beheaded and one woman was burnt at the stake.

HANGED, DRAWN AND QUARTERED

This particularly gruesome form of execution was the statutory death penalty for men convicted of high treason. Those convicted were first hanged, although the hangman was careful not to snap the neck but to simply strangle the unfortunate victim until he was nearly dead. Then he would be disembowelled: his belly was slit open and his intestines pulled out. If he was lucky then at this stage the shock and agony might kill him, or he might linger until he was beheaded. Finally, his body would be cut into quarters. All the pieces or perhaps just the head would be prominently displayed (in London, it was usually on London Bridge).

A nobleman might be given a more honourable end and simply be beheaded. Amazingly, a sense of public decency decreed that this sort of treatment should not be administered to a woman. They were burned at the stake instead.

These ghastly rituals were always public spectacles. Huge crowds would turn up to watch and cheer. Mothers would bring their small children and babies and lift them up so that they would not miss any of the fun.

Hanged, drawn and quartered – a hideous punishment from history which was still in use as late as the nineteenth century. (LC-USZ62-119891)

AD 1735

THE HADLEIGH GANG

THROUGHOUT THE EIGHTEENTH century, smugglers were active on almost every beach and estuary along the coast of Suffolk. Fishing was the major business of the ports of Lowestoft, Southwold and Aldeburgh and when the fish moved to other waters, many of the fishermen turned to smuggling. For other men of the sea, smuggling was virtually a full-time occupation. The imposition of heavy taxes and duties on seaborne goods made smuggling profitable and inevitable. These were harsh economic times and for many men it was the difference between seeing their families eat or starve.

However, one of the biggest gangs of smugglers to be based in Suffolk were not from any of the major ports: they were men of Hadleigh, which was some 40 miles inland. At its height, the gang was 100 strong and each man would provide two horses for the task of carrying the contraband of tobacco, tea casks and brandy barrels inland from the beaches. The cargo would be unloaded from large ships on to smaller boats and then brought ashore at Leiston. Today the coastline here is quite flat but two centuries ago, there were spectacular cliffs breached by the Sizewell Gap, which made a convenient and secluded landing place.

The gang had a storehouse at the village of Semer on the little River Brett between Hadleigh and Stowmarket. On dark, moonless nights the line of packhorses would emerge from the gloom and unload the illicit goods at the safe house until they could be moved on again to the paying customers. It was a massive, well-organised operation, but eventually the location of the storehouse was discovered and a large force of dragoons and customs authorities made a sudden raid and seized it all.

The huge cache of contraband was moved to the George Inn at Hadleigh, but it was not to stay there for long. The smugglers were a force strong enough to make their own laws, or at least to disregard those of the authorities. In the middle of the night a gang of twenty men, armed and determined, soon arrived at the George and demanded the return of their rightful property. In the pitched battle that followed, one dragoon was shot dead and several others injured before the gang rode off into the darkness.

They took with them the chests, bales and brandy barrels that the customs men had tried to confiscate.

A number of the smugglers were recognised during the conflict and two of them were later caught and hanged for the crime of discharging their pistols. The leader of the gang was a man named John Harvey who was also caught, lodged for a while in Newgate Prison, and eventually transported. However, the gang elected a new leader and carried on as before. The next time one of their shipments fell into the hands of the authorities, they again had the nerve to break into the king's warehouse in Ipswich and steal it back.

The bravado of the Suffolk smugglers takes some beating. In another incident, 300 barrels of gin were landed at Leiston and quickly concealed in an old barn. This was one of the rare occasions when an informer promptly passed the word to the revenue men, no doubt hoping for a reward. The authorities duly arrived at the barn and were met by three of the smugglers, who stalled them with claims of innocence and arguments, while twenty of their pals chained the gin barrels out through an adjoining hay loft and on to a line of waiting carts behind the barn. When the barn was empty, the revenue men were allowed inside and the door was promptly locked behind them.

The gin was literally 'spirited' away to another hiding place, this time a cellar underneath a concealing dung heap. When the coast was clear, the smugglers came back to reclaim their goods. They cleared the dung back from the hatch but were in too much of a hurry to let the foul fumes clear away. Three of them went straight down to check on the barrels, and two of them were overcome by the unwholesome air and died.

'WATCH THE WALL, MY DARLING'

When smuggling was at its height, whole communities were often involved, or at least turned a blind eye. Kipling's advice to 'watch the wall, my darling, as the gentlemen go by' was the unspoken catchphrase of the day. In Aldeburgh it was once said that everybody in the port was involved except the parson.

Elsewhere in Suffolk, there were plenty of country vicars and parsons who had no such scruples. Contraband was hidden behind many church altars or underneath the pews. Almost everyone, it seemed, was on the side of the smuggler. Millers would set their sails at certain angles to signal whether or not the coast was clear. Shore or riverside pubs would set a lighted lantern or some sort of signal in their windows to carry the same warning.

Often dragoons would be billeted in the same inns used by the smugglers and publicans would keep a delicate balance between the two. If the dragoons were called out to help apprehend a group of smugglers, a smiling landlady would often offer them 'one for the road'. By the time the troopers eventually reported for duty, they would be too late and often too inebriated to take any useful action.

AD 1759

REDCOATS, RED ROSES, AND RAW RED COURAGE

FOR THE BEST part of three centuries, Suffolk soldiers have fought and campaigned over every far-flung corner of the globe. The Suffolk Regiment was formed in 1685, when King James II called for more troops to protect him from the threatened Monmouth Rebellion. In the event, by the time they were formed they were not needed, but the Suffolk soldiers have been in the thick of every conflict of empire ever since.

The Suffolk soldier. (Royal Anglian Regiment Museum)

In 1690, in brilliant red coats and carrying matchlock rifles, the Suffolk Regiment was in Ireland on the first of its many overseas postings, helping to storm Carrickfergus Castle, and fighting in the Battle of the Boyne. William of Orange, the ruler of the Protestant Dutch, had married Princess Mary (the daughter of James II) to become King of England. He had arrived with a Dutch Army and without a shot being fired in what became known as the Glorious Revolution. However, the King of France backed the Catholics in Ireland and William was forced to fight them. He needed the doughty Suffolk soldiers, although it was a victory that was to be a thorn in the side of every English monarch who came after him.

In the years that followed, the ever-growing list of the Suffolk Regiment battle honours reads like the pages of a world gazette: France, Gibraltar, India, South Africa, New Zealand, Afghanistan, Greece, Egypt, Palestine, Malaya, Burma. Wherever the British Army was required to fight, the Suffolk soldiers were there, doing their glorious bit for King (or Queen) and Country.

On 1 August 1759 they were at the Battle of Minden, one of the major battles of the Seven Years War. William Pitt, the British prime minister, had sent British troops to support Frederick the Great of Prussia against the French. Pitt's reasoning was that by helping to tie up large numbers of French troops, he would make progress easier for England's colonial ambitions in Canada and India. He may well have been right, because Quebec was eventually taken by General Wolfe, winning Canada from the French.

Gibraltar Barracks in Bury St Edmunds, the home of the Suffolk soldier.

THE GRAND SORTIE

Ten years later, the Suffolk Regiment was in Gibraltar, ready to defend the colony in the Great Siege by the forces of France and Spain, which they broke by carrying the fight to the enemy with a magnificent Grand Sortie on 17 November 1781. There they earned the right to take the arms of Gibraltar, the insignia of its castle and key, to be worn thereafter in their cap badges and colours.

In 1796 the regiment landed for the first time in India, and soon the red-coated tide of its fighting men distinguished themselves yet again, this time at Seringapatam, overwhelming the rebel stronghold of Tipoo Sultan, the ruler of Mysore. Over the next hundred years the regiment's battalions were constantly in action in India, South Africa, and Afghanistan. Wherever the British flag flew, the Suffolks fought to keep it flying.

'WOMEN AND CHILDREN FIRST'

However, the finest moments of the Suffolk soldiers were not always in the heat of battle, for even in the face of disaster their courage and discipline stood firm. When HMS *Birkenhead* was shipwrecked off the Cape coast in 1852, she carried a draft of seventy privates and one sergeant, on their way to join their battalion in South Africa. The men paraded on deck and stood by while the women and children were given the few places in the lifeboats. Most of these men drowned when the ship went down. A marble roll of honour commemorates this event in the regimental chapel in St Mary's church in Bury St Edmunds, and the order of the day – 'Women and children first' – has gone down in history.

Minden was a fortified city on the River Weser in Germany, and the French and British sides lined up their cavalry, artillery and infantry regiments on the plain in front of the city. The French Army consisted of 10,000 cavalry and 30,000 infantry, altogether some 44,000 men. The combined British and German forces numbered 37,000. The battle began with an artillery duel on one flank, but the decisive action was fought in the centre.

Somehow down the chain of command, orders on the allied side became confused. The infantry of the British contingent in the centre were meant to form in line ready to advance when so ordered, but they received an order *to* advance to the beating of the drums. The men may have sworn a little bit, but they were well trained and disciplined. To the amazement of the senior commanders on both sides, the drums sounded and the British soldiers advanced, straight into the ranks of the French cavalry and the heart of the main French Army.

The Suffolk Regiment was among the six British regiments that marched and fought through murderous cannon fire at Minden. Three French cavalry charges broke and floundered upon the close-packed ranks of the British redcoats. The British regiments should have been doomed, but they just got on with the job and kept going forward. Pure courage and steady musket fire cut down the enemy horses and riders, and turned the plain into a killing ground. Finally the redcoats smashed into the blue of the French infantry and the Frenchmen fled the field.

The British had won the most splendid infantry victory of any war. The French commander Contades is reported to have said bitterly, 'I have seen what I never thought to be possible, a single line of infantry break through three lines of cavalry, ranked in order of battle, and tumble them to ruin!'

On that bright spring day, the hedgerows around Minden had been filled with flowering red and yellow roses. As they advanced, the doughty Suffolk men displayed a flamboyant bravado, plucking red and yellow blossoms and wearing them jauntily in their hats. Today their successors still wear the red and yellow roses on 1 August to commemorate the anniversary of their triumph.

FOUR HEADLESS HORSES

SUFFOLK HAS HAD more than its fair share of ghosts and hauntings. The abbey ruins at Bury St Edmunds are said to be haunted by the ghost of St Edmund, as well as a Brown Monk and a Grey Lady. At Icklingham, about 8 miles north west of Bury, is a small hill on a heath called Deadman's Grave. A horse rider was buried here after being thrown from his mount and killed. Obviously he was annoyed at his bad luck, so his ghost lurks in the shadows and frightens all other horses after nightfall.

At Kentford there is a gypsy boy's grave beside the crossroads on the main road to Bury. The boy is said to have committed suicide rather than be hanged for a false charge of sheep stealing. Some strange force emanating from the grave is now said to have toppled some cyclists from their bikes as they pass the fateful spot.

Great Livermere, just north of Bury, has been called the most haunted village in England. A strange lady in red who has the malicious habit of terrifying drivers at night by suddenly stepping out in front of their oncoming cars seems to head the hierarchy, although several other ghostly manifestations have been reported. A phantom cyclist also pedals around the country roads at night.

One particularly gruesome tale is of two gypsy half-brothers, who fought a terrible knife duel to the death at Sibton Green. Both were sons of the head of the gypsy clan, but the illegitimate one was favoured by his father and a murderous hatred grew between them. They settled it one night in a fight so vicious that both of them bled to death from the savage knife wounds they had inflicted on each other.

The bodies were found at dawn, sprawled lifeless on the gore-sodden grass at the edge of the green with their bloodied knives beside them. The people of the village were shocked and startled by the scene and initially there was no explanation. At the nearby gypsy camp, the caravan doors were all shut and the curtains drawn, and no one would speak. If the gypsies had watched two of their number in mortal combat, no one would say. Hints of the cause of the fight slowly emerged much later.

The bodies were buried close by where they were found and inevitably the spot was seen as tainted by evil. There were tales of luminous ghostly faces floating beneath the trees where the leaves dripped blood. A schoolmaster who considered himself above the normal village superstitions ventured into the wood and came out half insane, refusing to speak of what he had seen.

And if that tale is not gruesome enough, here is another. Many parts of England have tales of a headless horseman who rides on dark, stormy nights, but Suffolk goes one better. Between Southwold and Bungay travels a phantom coach pulled by four headless horses. One story tells of the rivalry between a coachman and a carter from Southwold, and of a lonely road through two great banks of holly hedges that threw fearsome black shadows. On pitch-black nights, horses would shy away from that black road and could only be forced past with a great show of reluctance. The carter who carried the fish catches inland from Southwold docks in his unlit cart was afraid of that dreadful road. His rival, who drove a smart liveried coach with bright shining lanterns, was not.

On one particularly foul black night, the driving rain forced the carter to take a short cut home down that grim road. As he penetrated the black tunnel between the hedges, his horse began to hesitate and stopped several times. The animal was clearly spooked, its nostrils quivering as it sensed something strange. Suddenly a coach began to take shape in the gloom. It was illuminated by its own lamps. The driver sat erect in his box, wearing clothes of an earlier age. His four horses were all headless, the necks ending in bloody stumps.

BLACK SHUCK, THE DEVIL'S DOG

Bungay is a thriving little town with plenty of interest in the castle ruins and several fine churches. Central Saint Mary's with its dominating square flint tower is where the famous Black Dog of Bungay burst in upon a terrified congregation on one stormy Sunday in 1577.

The day had started bright and sunny as the congregation made their way to the church, but by the time they had assembled inside the storm had descended and the day had become as black as the darkest night. It was the most ferocious storm they had ever known, with terrifying claps of thunder and vivid streaks of lightning splitting the rain-slashed skies. The good folk of Bungay cowered in their holy refuge as the storm raged outside, but the church was no protection.

Suddenly a mighty crash of thunder and a howling burst of wind blasted the doors open. Through them came hurtling a huge black beast, which could best be described as a monstrous devil dog. Lightning flashes seared through the gloom as the beast rampaged up and down the aisles and between the pews. The monster hound killed two of their number and the event was firmly believed to be a visitation from 'Black Shuck', the Devil's dog.

On the same fateful day, what seems to have been the same supernatural storm struck at the coastal town of Blytheborough. Again the church was the chosen target and again the closed doors were torn open by the screaming winds. The black beast repeated its terrifying performance and the horrified congregation saw two of their number killed before the creature withdrew.

The carter's horse pulled back in the shafts in terror. The cart stopped and the carter stared in horror. Just as suddenly, the phantom coach began to move. It pulled away down the lane and vanished. The carter told his tale in his local pub and his coachman friend laughed him down, accusing him of having partaken of too much ale before he encountered the ghostly coach. The outcome of the exchange was that the coachman volunteered to escort the carter through the ghostly lane the next time they were both due to travel that way.

A few nights later, the fish cart duly followed the brightly lit coach into the black tunnel through the hedgerows. The night was fitfully moonlit through heavy passing clouds, so sometimes the lighted coach was visible in the gloom and sometimes it was not. The coachman kept calling back taunts and encouragement, but then went strangely silent.

The fish cart finally emerged from the lane. The coach ahead had pulled aside to let him pass, its driver acknowledging the carter with a wave of his hand. The coach was already turning, so the carter did not see the horses as they disappeared back into the lane.

He never knew which coach he had actually followed through the lane. The coach his mocking friend had driven was later pulled empty into the Southwold pub yard by its sweating, quivering horse. The disbelieving coachman was found dead on the side of the haunted lane with a look of horror upon his face.

AD 1915

BEYOND THE CALL OF DUTY

WHILE THE AIR and sea defences were put to the test, men of all ages rallied to the call to fight. In Europe, the war soon bogged down into the terrible stalemate of the trenches. When advances were made, men were cut to shreds by merciless machine-gun fire. When they sheltered or half drowned in the stinking mud of the trenches, they were picked off by sniper fire or choked to death by poison gas attacks. Men who had lost their gas masks desperately urinated into handkerchiefs that they pressed over their faces.

This was the terrible new face of twentieth-century warfare and the place names Ypres, Loos, Flanders and the Somme will forever evoke images of dogged mud and blood-soaked bravery and pure senseless carnage. For their part, the Suffolk Regiment formed a total of twenty-three battalions and took part in every major battle of the war, earning eighty-one battle honours. Among over 300 awards for gallantry, two Victoria Crosses were won, the first by Sergeant Arthur Frederick Saunders of the 9th Battalion at Loos in September of 1915, and the second by Corporal Sydney James Day at Peronne in 1917.

The 9th Battalion had marched through several nights of pouring rain to reach the battlefield and were not expecting to go into action until they had rested. However, they were thrown straight into supporting the Scottish regiments, who were already making an attack.

After his battalion had been forced to retire and his officer had been wounded, Sergeant Saunders won his VC by taking charge of two machine guns and a handful of men, despite a severe thigh wound which eventually shortened his leg. He closely supported the last four charges of the Cameron Highlanders as they attacked and tried to overwhelm the

Early model gas mask in the trenches, September 1915. (THP)

German trenches. When that battalion was also forced to retire, Saunders stuck to his machine guns, still giving orders and maintaining continuous fire to cover their retirement.

In the horror and madness of the battlefield, accounts get confused, but now it was the Germans who were advancing. A second lieutenant of the Cameron Highlanders later reported that he lay wounded in a shell hole and was appalled to see the British forces pulling back on either side of him. Suddenly a British sergeant with a bloodied leg and Lewis machine gun tumbled into the shell hole beside him. It was Arthur Saunders. As a wave of German soldiers came toward them Arthur opened up again with the Lewis gun and the Germans were driven back.

Stretcher-bearers picked up the two wounded men but, under heavy shell fire, were forced to abandon them again. They survived to be picked up by a second stretcher party and eventually reached a dressing station. Some accounts say that here Arthur's leg was amputated but it was in fact saved and he spent the rest of his life with one leg 3in shorter than the other. Arthur Saunders eventually returned to his hometown of Ipswich, to a stupendous hero's welcome.

Corporal Day won his award for leading a bombing section detailed to clear a maze of trenches still held by the enemy. In the process he killed two machine-gunners and took four prisoner. When a German stick bomb landed in a trench where there were five other British soldiers, Day grabbed it and threw it back a split second before it exploded. With the trench cleared he finally established himself in an advanced position and remained at his post for sixty-six hours under heavy shell, grenade and rifle fire.

The nightmare thunder of these massive battles in France could often be heard on the Suffolk coast. The sounds undoubtedly spurred on all those who were working at home on the war effort. Garrets at Leiston had transformed their production lines to manufacturing aeroplanes. In the fields, the Women's Land Army was filling some of the gaps left by the men at the front. Bicycle battalions of volunteers and special constables patrolled the roads and searched the skies for the drone of Zeppelin engines.

When the war ended, memorials sprouted in every town and village to commemorate the long lists of names of those who had never returned from the colossal waste of life in Europe.

Going over the top in the trenches. (THP)

AD 1917

ZEPPELINS OVER SUFFOLK

The pistol shots that started the First World War were fired upon a street in Sarajevo in June 1914. The assassination of a previously unknown archduke by an unheard-of Serbian terrorist was to have monumental consequences and ultimately cause the deaths of 8.5 million people. Those shots were the spark that ignited global tensions and precipitated the entry of the Great Powers of Europe into the First World War.

Franz Ferdinand and his family; his death was the spark that ignited the First World War. (Library of Congress, George Grantham Bain Collection, LC-DIG-GGBAIN-15555)

Suffolk and Norfolk were the nearest counties to Europe, separated only by the English Channel, and so the coastline of East Anglia was in effect the front line. Invasion was feared and defence lines were created with trenches and pill boxes. Mobile artillery was brought in to supplement the few fixed gun batteries, and Landguard Fort at Felixstowe was made ready. Since the Napoleonic wars it had always been expected that one day the country would have to repel the French, but now it was the Germans, the Implacable Hun, who were the enemy.

Winged aircraft were in their biplane infancy and so it was the airships, the dreaded Zeppelins, which were the first cause for concern. Second were the new-fangled and cowardly submarines, which could massacre merchant shipping with their machine guns and then hide beneath the waves.

Both threats led to a wave of spy mania, as it was feared that traitors with torches or even car headlights could be passing signals to overhead airships or to submarines out at sea, telling them where to drop their bombs or direct their fire. In the end, no actual spies were ever discovered.

April 1916 brought the Battle of Lowestoft, when a German battle cruiser squadron appeared to bombard the ports of Lowestoft, which was being used for minelaying and minesweeping operations, and Great Yarmouth, a base for British submarines. The bombardment seems to have been an attempt to draw out the defending British ships, which would then have been sunk. The smaller British ships refused to take the bait, however.

The guns from four German battle cruisers pounded Lowestoft and destroyed 200 houses and two shore gun

Royal Hotel and pier, Lowestoft; the town was struck by bombs during the First World War. (LC-DIG-PPMSC-08616)

The Sopwith Camel: these gallant little biplanes flew up to challenge the Zeppelins.

batteries. Twelve people were injured and three were killed. The damage could have been worse if thick fog had not obscured the gunners' aim. The German ships withdrew when a British squadron of battle cruisers moved to meet them: the German aim was to cut off small sections of the British fleet and sink them, not to lose ships of their own.

More serious were the bombing raids by the German airships. On 19 January 1915, the first airship had appeared over Lowestoft. It was one of three that had failed to find their intended targets, but the bright lights of Lowestoft were impossible to miss, especially with navigation helped by the shining beacon of Happisburgh Lightship. Later the blackout would be enforced, but the lightship was never moved because it was vital to the coastal trade of British ships.

The Zeppelin L5 dropped six high-explosive and forty incendiary bombs on Lowestoft and Southwold as it made its terrible flight over the coast of Suffolk. A Lowestoft timber yard was hit and the stacks of dry timber were easy to ignite. The yard was promptly destroyed by fire.

Later raids up and down the Norfolk and Suffolk coast saw bombs and incendiaries dropped again on Lowestoft in support of the naval attack, on Ipswich and Woodbridge, and as far inland as Bury St Edmunds. In 1917 Felixstowe was attacked and bombed by German seaplanes. Numerous villages were also bombed or suffered near misses. Airship navigation was difficult and all too often the Zeppelin commanders simply dropped their loads wherever they happened to be when it was time to turn around and head for home. London was just within their range but the Kaiser had given orders that the English Royal Family must not be harmed. They were, after all, his cousins.

An airship in flames. (LC-DIG-ggbain-14727)

That left East Anglia to take the brunt of the airship attacks.

The superior heights to which the airships could climb put them above the ceiling of the gallant little biplanes of the Royal Flying Corps which sailed up to meet them, but the gas-filled dirigibles did not have things all their own way. Some were hit by anti-aircraft fire and others shot down by machine-gun fire from fighter planes when circumstances forced them to lose height.

The night of 16 June 1917 saw the most dramatic conflagration of Suffolk's history. A fleet of six Zeppelins had been despatched to raid southern England. Only two successfully completed the sea crossing and one of those, the ill-fated L48, arrived over the Suffolk coast. It failed to find its intended target, which was Harwich, and instead dodged anti-aircraft batteries and searchlights to drop bombs on Martlesham, Fakenham and Kirton.

As it passed over Leiston, the L48 was at last caught in the British searchlights on the ground below. She was hotly pursued by three RFC biplanes and with her engines failing, her compass frozen and her rudder damaged, the airship was losing height in the hope of dropping into a favourable tailwind.

The three British fighters tore into her in turn, with their Lewis machine guns spitting bright red flashes of tracer fire. The airship was still above them and most of the ammunition expended by the first two pilots failed to reach the target. The third plane got closer and the incendiary bullets ripped into the giant hydrogen gas balloon. At first a small fire started in the stern of the airship, but quickly its glow expanded to turn the whole ship into a fantastic Chinese lantern illuminated from within. Then the Zeppelin exploded and crumbled in a gigantic falling mass of flame.

Its plummeting death fall was visible from 50 miles away as it crashed to earth near the tiny village of Theberton. Some of the doomed crew were seen struggling out of their heavy leather jackets and uniforms, presumably believing that they were over the sea and might have a chance to swim for their lives. It was not to be and they were all killed in the impact.

AD 1922

SHIPWRECK AND STORM

Suffolk has roughly 50 miles of coastline as the seagull flies, plus a bit more if you count round all the bays and headlands. However precise you want to be, the harsh North Sea still makes a cold and sometimes ferocious neighbour. Many ships have been lost and many sailors drowned in wrecks on its sandbars and shoals. Sailors are a hardy breed and they do not leave their fellow sailors to the sea if they can help it. So, in 1801, the lifeboat station was established in the port of Lowestoft.

Hundreds of lives have been saved in the years since, but one rescue will have to suffice here to illustrate the bravery and determination of all the others. In 1922 the steam merchant ship *Hopelyn* set sail from Newcastle. She was a 2,348-ton vessel, 285ft long with a crew of twenty-four men and one ship's cat named Tiffy. The ship's cat was important in those days: an essential crewmember with the job of keeping the ship's rats under control.

The *Hopelyn* was bound for London with a cargo of coal. What else would you carry from Newcastle? On the way she encountered a powerful north-easterly gale. This was nothing unusual in the wild North Sea, but the *Hopelyn* had more bad luck: her steering gear broke down. Desperate temporary repairs were made but the storm conditions grew even more furious and the repairs failed to hold. The *Hopelyn* was out of control and at the mercy of the storm. The mountainous rolling seas drove her savagely on to Scroby Sands.

The great shifting sandbars off the Suffolk and Norfolk coast had been the death trap and graveyard for many sailors and ships. Now it was the *Hopelyn's* turn to be stranded, held fast and pounded by the merciless waves. Under the relentless hammering of the seas, the ship began to break up.

An urgent mayday was broadcast before the radio mast was torn away by the screaming wind. The crew gathered on the bridge, the highest part of the superstructure, but still the waves reared up to terrify them. They scrambled even higher to the tiny radio shack where they could go no further, and there, no doubt, they prayed. The mayday signal was heard and the lifeboat *Kentwell* from Gorleston was launched. The *Kentwell* was powered by sail and oars, but her

THE ALDEBURGH DISASTER

The Aldeburgh lifeboats have an equally impressive record of hundreds of souls saved from the hungry sea, but also of one terrible disaster when the sea took its revenge and six Aldeburgh lifeboat men were lost.

It happened in 1899. The small boats that made their living fishing for sprat had left Aldeburgh harbour on the morning tide. A sudden storm sprang up and caught them at sea. Those who had gone north saw the dark clouds brewing and managed to put in to Sizewell beach. Others who had gone south were caught far offshore as the thunderclouds hurtled down upon them. By midday a full gale was raging; the boats were in danger of being overwhelmed and were firing distress signals to call for help.

The alarm gun was fired to assemble the lifeboat crew. Both her coxswain and her second coxswain were sick and unable to sail which caused some delay, but as swiftly as possible the boat was launched into the pounding breakers that roared up the beach.

Launching the Aldeburgh lifeboat today.

With difficulty, the boat was rowed offshore and the foresail hoisted. The boat turned south and raced to the rescue of the small fishing boats. Then, in full view of the crowds lining the beach, disaster struck. As she ran over the shoal through heavy seas, one massive wave struck her on the quarter. Before the helm could recover another huge sea hit her broadside and turned her over.

Most of her crew of eighteen managed to swim the 150 yards to the shore in their lifejackets, but six men were trapped underneath the boat as it rolled. The upturned boat was thrown into the shallows by the spiteful sea. There it was rolled back and forth, grinding through the wave-lashed shingle as men made frantic efforts to reach their crewmates. By the time they were retrieved, the six men had all drowned.

coxswain had acquired a tow from the tug *George Jewson* and the two boats set out together into a howling black night filled with 40ft waves.

When they reached the sands, the *Kentwell* fired off flares to light up the *Hopelyn*'s position. The crews saw to their dismay that the freighter's back was already broken and only a small part of the ship was still visible above the waves. Any hopes that the skipper of the *George Jewson* had for salvage were gone. Coxswain Billy Fleming and his crew on the *Kentwell* peered through the nightmare of pouring rain and heaving seas but could see no signs of life on the stricken ship. Their hopes of affecting a rescue also seemed dashed.

The *Kentwell* held her position until dawn, but still there was no sign of life. They had to assume that the crew had either perished or somehow left the ship and reluctantly returned to shore. Within an hour, however, they learned that a signal flag had been spotted, tied to the funnel of the *Hopelyn*. There had been no flag on the funnel when they left. Somehow, someone was still alive on the disintegrating ship. Billy Fleming and his crew went back.

The storm was still raging. The *Kentwell* battled her way through the waves but as they closed with the wreck, a huge wave smashed the lifeboat against the freighter's hull. Fleming had to untangle his boat and get her clear of the wreck and the sands. The *Kentwell* was so badly damaged and at risk of sinking that Fleming had to take her back to the shore once again.

At this stage the Lowestoft lifeboat, the *Agnes Cross*, with coxswain Jack Swan at the helm, was called out to take over the rescue. The two lifeboats passed at sea and Billy Fleming transferred to the Lowestoft boat to help guide her out to the wreck. They reached the *Hopelyn* but again darkness was closing in. The storm would not let up and the foul conditions eventually forced the *Agnes Cross* to abandon the effort and return to shore. But the rescuers were not giving up. At dawn on the following day the *Agnes Cross* sailed again, with both coxswains and a mixed crew of the strongest men from both lifeboats. The gale was still blowing fiercely but this time coxswain Swan manoeuvred his boat alongside the wreck and in thirty minutes of death-defying work, all twenty-four of the freighter's crew scrambled down ropes from the tiny wireless room and reached the safety of the lifeboat's deck.

One of the rescued crewmen carefully cradled the terrified Tiffy tucked inside his coat. After the combined efforts of two lifeboats and thirty-two hours of storm and despair, even the ship's cat had been saved.

THE SILVER DARLINGS

The silver age of the herring lasted from Norman times until the mid-1930s, when King Herring at last virtually vanished from the cold North Sea. The great silver shoals would arrive off the North Norfolk coast every autumn, seemingly as certain as the red-gold leaves that marked the end of every summer, but sadly they could not survive over-fishing by the vast fleets of steam drifters and trawlers that were converging upon Lowestoft and Great Yarmouth. Lowestoft had a huge fleet of boats working from its crowded quays and jetties and the rivalry between the Yarmouth and the Lowestoft crews became almost legendary.

After 1,000 years, the catches dwindled until the quicksilver shoals were gone.

Eventually, in the glorious heyday of the herring fishing industry in the latter part of the nineteenth century, there would be around 12,000 fishermen and boys working in the gale-lashed waters of the harsh North Sea. The boats sailed and fished in fleets of fifty or more smacks and trawlers, and could be away for two months at a time. They trawled at night, hauled up the catch around dawn, and then transferred it to faster carrier boats which then raced the ice-packed silver harvest to port where it could be sold as quickly and as fresh as possible. The fishing fleet stayed out in the cold, grey wastes of water to carry on their hard and freezing tasks of trawling and hauling.

It was a cruel, harsh life, with men frequently washed overboard and lost either in the vicious gales, or during the dangerous task of transferring the fish boxes from one boat to another. On average a fisherman was lost at the rate of one a day from 1880 to 1890.

As it might have been; fishing smacks rally off Southwold.

AD 1938

THE SECOND WORLD WAR

WHEN NAZI GERMANY occupied a large part of Czechoslovakia in 1938, Adolf Hitler promised Neville Chamberlain and other European leaders that this was to be the limit of Germany's territorial demands. The duped British prime minister came home from the Munich Agreement triumphantly waving a piece of paper that he claimed meant 'Peace for our time'. But the ink was barely dry on this worthless document when the German Army resumed its storming progress through the rest of Czechoslovakia, Poland, and on into Western Europe. The Second World War had begun.

As one of the counties nearest to the Continental mainland, Suffolk was again on the front line. The initial German air attacks were upon British shipping in the North Sea, but soon the bombing attacks began. The main target of the Luftwaffe was the almighty Blitz upon London, but stray bombers also found time to bomb Bury St Edmunds, Newmarket, Ipswich and Felixstowe. One of the most devastating air raids of the entire war happened in August of 1940 when 100 German bombers took part in a massive raid on the British fighter base at Martlesham.

The war years began with renewed fears of a massive land invasion from the sea, but the main focus of the conflict soon became the skies above. Existing airfields were expanded and new airfields established until the whole land mass of East Anglia was virtually one great aircraft carrier. The Battle of Britain was fought and won by the valiant few in their Spitfires and Hurricanes as furious dogfights filled the Suffolk skies. The tide was turned and then the aerial battlefields were forced back over Europe.

The Americans came in their thousands to back up our own Lancaster and Liberator bombers in this new phase of the aerial war against Hitler. Rougham Airfield is one of the many East Anglian airfields from which the Mighty Eighth US Air Force flew during the Second World War. It was built on the flat Suffolk farm fields in 1942 and briefly occupied by the 322nd Bomb Group with their B-26 Marauders. These were later replaced by the 94th Bomb Group with their famous B-17s. This model is better known as the revolutionary Flying Fortress, the first all-metal, four-engine monoplane, with bristling gun turrets.

The old control tower at Rougham Airfield.

The mighty Flying Fortress.

Those were the days when the sight of the planes and the sound of their engines continuously filled the skies over Suffolk. The 94th flew 324 missions over enemy-occupied Europe. They roared out in defiant close formations, and limped home in smaller, fragmented groups; some of them trailing smoke, many of them never reappearing at all.

The nearby Rattlesden Airfield was opened in 1942 with three massive wartime runways forming a giant triangle. It became the wartime home of the USAF 447th Bomb Group, also part of the Mighty Eighth, flying a fleet of thundering B-17s with laconic nicknames like the Squirming Squaw, The Ground Pounder, Rowdy Rebel and Ol' Scrapiron. Between the dark and bloody days from December 1943 and April 1945, they flew 258 combat missions over occupied Europe and Nazi Germany, comprising 8,229 individual flights.

These are just two examples of the scores of airfields established in Suffolk and Norfolk. Their initial task was to prepare for the Allied invasion of Europe by relentlessly bombing the enemy airfields and missile sites, their naval installations and submarine pens,

TOP SECRET WORK AT BAWDSEY MANOR

In those dark days Bawdsey Manor, which overlooks a shingle beach and the North Sea near the mouth of the River Deben, was occupied by the Air Ministry. This lovely old green-turreted mansion has nine towers, supposedly one for each of the millions of pounds made by its builder, Sir Cuthbert Quilter, who had amassed his fortune in the city. Here the top-secret research work that resulted in the invention of radar was accomplished. Thanks to this invaluable work, the fighter pilots of the RAF had been able to hold off the vastly superior numbers of the German Luftwaffe, and so win the Battle of Britain.

From that beginning, the reconquest of Europe had become possible and almost certainly helped Britain and her allies to win the Second World War.

the great railway marshalling yards, factories and cities and anything that could damage the enemy morale and war effort. After D-Day, the motivation shifted to pounding the enemy positions in advance of the beach-heads and aiding the breakout of the Allied armies.

On the ground, food rationing was soon introduced. Winston Churchill had replaced Neville Chamberlain as prime minister; Great Britain now had a bulldog war leader instead of a pacifist appeaser.

The composition of the population had shifted. The young men were fighting on foreign battlefronts. The older men and any others left behind had formed the Home Guard, now fondly remembered by *Dad's Army*. Women and children had been evacuated from the coastal areas, while thousands of evacuees from London had flooded into the inland areas. Women everywhere were playing their part in the war effort. The Women's Land Army had been revived and volunteers were pitching straw and driving tractors. Young single women were being called up to help man anti-aircraft batteries, fill military desk jobs and airfield control centres.

E-BOAT ALLEY

Throughout the war, the Germans operated large fleets of small, fast motor torpedo and gunboats in the English Channel and the North Sea. Their task was to sink as much English shipping as possible in lightning hit-and-run attacks. The Germans called them S-boats, the S standing for *Schnellboot* ('fastboat' in English). To the English they were E-boats, E for enemy. The sea off the Suffolk coast and their general area of operations became known as E-Boat Alley.

The Air Force base at Felixstowe which had previously flown seaplanes was handed over to the Royal Naval Coastal Force and became HMS *Beehive*, a major base for one of the flotillas of British motor torpedo boats, motor gunboats, and motor launches that were deployed to combat the ravages of the E-boats. The base also continued to fly short Sunderland flying boats, which were engaged in rescuing shot down British pilots.

The E-boats generally preyed upon the British ship convoys at night, using the cover of darkness. As night fell, the British boats would also begin their patrols, ready to intercept and destroy the enemy.

The E-boats are credited with the sinking of more than 100 merchant ships, together with a large assortment of navy ships including twelve destroyers, eleven minesweepers and a submarine. The Navy's 'little ships', as the flotillas became affectionately known, sank more than 400 German ships, including forty-eight E-boats. They were part of that great armada of little ships – the fishing boats, the pleasure boats and anything else that would float – which took part in the evacuation of Dunkirk. The flotillas were back in force to support the D-Day landings and the invasion of Europe, but 170 of the 'little ships' paid the ultimate price and were destroyed.

When the war ended, the Nazi Admiral Karl Bruening was faced with the ignominious task of making the formal surrender of his E-boat fleet to the Commander of the British base at Felixstowe.

AD 1943

THE RAILWAY OF DEATH

MEANWHILE, OUR SUFFOLK soldiers were in the thick of the fighting in Europe and beyond. The First Battalion of the Suffolk Regiment formed part of the British Expeditionary Force that had to be evacuated at Dunkirk, but they were back again on 6 June 1944, storming Sword Beach in Normandy as part of the Assault Brigade. This time they were there to stay, fighting their way through France, Belgium, the Netherlands, and then the German heartland, until finally Hitler and his allies were decisively beaten.

The Second Battalion was stationed in India at the outbreak of the war, and in November of 1943 they were moved into Burma as part of the 'Forgotten' Fourteenth Army. There they fought the Japanese with the utmost skill and bravery, taking a notable part in the Arakan and Imphal campaigns. They, too, fought until the Japanese were finally defeated.

Singapore burning after a Japanese attack. (LC-DIG-DS-04803)

Further south, the Fourth and Fifth battalions fought equally gallantly in the defence of Singapore, but for once the indomitable Suffolk fighting spirit was not enough. With all her big guns facing the sea, Singapore was never designed to withstand an attack from the Malayan mainland, and was overwhelmed by the sheer weight of numbers of the enemy.

Most of the Suffolk soldiers were taken prisoner and many were forced to work on building the Burma railway, the infamous Railway of Death. The line was planned to run for 258 miles from Bangkok in Thailand to Rangoon in Burma to support the Japanese military campaign, which the Japanese hoped would pave the way for a thrust into India. It would be a supply route preferable to the longer sea lanes that were vulnerable to Allied air attack.

THE BODIES ON THE BEACH

Shingle Street was once a small fishing village on the Suffolk coast but now it has virtually vanished. In its place is a web of myth and mystery that has baffled and intrigued the local pub talk, the national press and the world-wide media ever since the end of the Second World War.

The facts are few and simple. After Britain's retreat from Europe and the evacuation at Dunkirk, the whole of Eastern England was filled with the fear of a massive German invasion and rumours ran riot. The inhabitants of Shingle Street were given just three days to evacuate their homes and the whole shoreline was cleared. Later an indeterminate number of German bodies were washed up on to the beach, some of them wearing British uniforms and many of them horribly burned.

The authorities maintained a tight-lipped silence. The Official Secrets Act tightened every nut and bolt on the facts of what had actually happened. Fact and fantasy flew wide on the wings of unchained speculation. The most popular theory was that an attempted German invasion had taken place. A flotilla of small boats had spearheaded the proposed invasion but had been caught and bombed by the RAF as it crossed the North Sea. Some boats had almost made it through but had encountered a new petroleum weapon: massive pipes from the shore spouting jets of blazing oil that had turned the waves into a sea of fire. This makes a good story that neatly explains the burned and bloated bodies that later rolled up in the tide. But why was there no major back up from the German Navy? When the Allied Armies did the proper job on D-Day, there was massive shelling from British warships as the troop carriers stormed in.

Okay, so Shingle Street was just a spearhead, perhaps aimed at a quick rush inland to secure Martlesham airbase only 10 miles away. With a captured airfield, troops could have been quickly flown in to expand the invasion. But this would have necessitated a large force of troop planes and soldiers on stand-by, and surely the German Navy would have been on support alert as soon as the initial surprise was lost. There is an argument that the Home Office suppressed all information on the incident because they did not want to incur panic by revealing how vulnerable we were and how close the invasion came. Similar arguments suggest that the German High Command imposed silence because they did not want to admit to a failure and show that they were not invincible. But is it really credible that with so many men involved all of them could be sworn to silence for the rest of their lives?

So perhaps this was just a small commando raid, which is popular theory No. 2. Shingle Street was only 3 miles north of Bawdsey Manor, where the top-secret radar project was being developed and perfected. It was also only 3 miles south of Orford Ness, another top-secret research centre where the War Office were busy with a variety of secret projects. Either site could have been the target for a lightning search-and-destroy raid, or perhaps it was a synchronised dual target attack to hit both research facilities at the same time. That could explain why some of the dead Germans were wearing British uniforms.

Orford Ness had a long history as secret military testing site, beginning during the First World War when part of this marshy spit of isolated coastline had been drained and levelled to build two airfields. Flood protection walls were built. New aircraft and new bomb- and machine-gun sights were tested, and various equipment and techniques were perfected under experimental conditions.

During the Second World War, Orford Ness was again a hive of top-secret activity, including petroleum warfare, or how to create an impenetrable barrage of flame on the high seas. Scientists from Portland Down were also experimenting with a bomb loaded with a mixture of liquid mustard and high explosive. They did carry out one 250lb-bomb run in 1943 using the Shingle Street pub, the Lifeboat Inn, as a target.

With all of this going on, Orford Ness must have been a high priority wartime target, either to put it out of action or to steal its secrets, or both.

So did the Germans try a commando raid that was wiped out by running into a wall of blazing fire? Or was there perhaps some kind of terrible accident during the highly volatile experiments with liquid mustard, high explosives, and burning oil? Was the act of sowing the sea with supposedly burned German bodies some kind of complex cover-up?

Or did nothing happen at all? Was it all stage managed? Could the whole inflated story be just a very clever propaganda exercise? The whole story of a failed German invasion valiantly repelled by an impregnable Britain soon circulated in triumphant whispers throughout England, Europe and America. It must have been a great morale-booster on the home front and in occupied Europe. It impressed the Americans and may have helped to bring them into the war.

Psychological warfare and the efficient use of propaganda can be just as useful as chemical and fire weapons in the task of winning victory. Seventy years on and we are still waiting for answers.

There had been plans for such a railway before the war, the route surveyed through jungle hills and crossing many rivers, but these had been abandoned because the route and conditions would prove too difficult. The Japanese High Command did not care. They had the answer. Helpless prisoners of war with no hope of escape and under the constant threat of machine guns would do the back-breaking work. Forced labour was the only way to build a railway in this killing heat and murderous terrain and 180,000 native labourers and 60,000 prisoners of war were used in its construction.

The tracks were laid through virgin jungle and hard rock passes under a blazing sun and in appalling conditions. The workers died of starvation, dysentery, cholera and exhaustion. Many of those who collapsed were simply beaten to death by their captors. Bridges were built and the tracks pushed forward for mile after bitter mile. Allied air attacks bombed the bridges, but the Japanese simply forced their virtual slaves to rebuild them.

In the end, 90,000 Asian labourers and over 12,000 Allied prisoners of war died as a result of this inhuman treatment. Captured, but never defeated, the Suffolk spirit of dignity and determination shone through it all. Many died, but some survived, although they were practically living skeletons. And in those intolerable and cruel conditions, survival itself was a victory.

AD 1953

STORM SURGE, THE FLOODS OF DEATH

THE SUFFOLK SHORELINE has always been subject to periodic rearrangement by the angry sea: remember Dunwich, Walberswick and Blythborough, the lost and near-vanished once great ports of the Middle Ages. On 31 January 1953, the sea drew in a great breath of storm and struck again.

It was the night of a high spring tide and two other fateful elements combined to turn it into a catastrophic disaster. Out in the wild North Sea, low atmospheric pressure had lifted up the water levels and powerful winds and gales drove it all southward through the narrowing funnel between the British Isles and Europe.

There was practically no advance warning as the huge storm wave smashed its way down the eastern coastline. While people in Scotland were drowning as they took the first impact of the surge, the inhabitants of coastal Suffolk were still enjoying their Saturday night pub chatter and dances. In those days there were no mobile phones, and in rural Suffolk the only early warning system was a frantically pedalling policeman on a bicycle.

The pitifully inadequate sea defences were breached everywhere and the sea roared into every estuary and inlet. They were monster seas – 2.5 metres higher than any ordinary spring tide – and they were unstoppable.

In Lowestoft the sea came over the top of the new sea walls and forced the River Lothing to breach its banks. Approximately 400 homes were flooded and forty children had to be rescued from a flooded church. As the storm surge rolled down the coastline, Southwold and Aldeburgh suffered in turn. In Southwold, five people drowned as the torrent swept away a row of houses in Ferry Road. However, the biggest disaster and the greatest loss of life occurred at low-lying Felixstowe. Miraculously the beach and promenade defences held, but the 140mph wind-driven tsunami found no barrier as it hurled into the double estuary of the Stour and the Orwell. It smashed down the flood walls of the Orwell and the floods surged into Felixstowe from behind.

The floods hit an estate of single-storey prefab houses. They were of flimsy construction, hastily erected as temporary housing after the war, and they stood no chance. The storm surge simply swept

The sea defences at Felixstowe today.

them off their foundations. The people inside were carried away screaming in their beds. Some of them managed to scramble desperately on to their heaving rooftops. In the cold, bitter, gale-lashed darkness of a black January night it was difficult to grasp the full horror of what was happening to them.

Fifty people died in Suffolk, forty-one of them drowning in the swirling floods that engulfed Felixstowe. It was four days before the floods receded, with further high tides every six hours. They were four days of heroic rescue work by thousands of volunteers. The Blitz spirit prevailed again as everyone rallied to help their neighbours. Every rowboat that could float was used to pluck those who were trapped from the hungry waters. Even the boats from Butlin's fun park were commandeered. The Red Cross provided first aid, food and refreshment in the hastily established rescue centre. American servicemen from the scattered USAF bases also pitched in to aid the great life-saving effort.

The terrifying wall of water that devastated the east coast was Britain's biggest ever peacetime disaster, but the people of Suffolk responded magnificently.

Lightning Source UK Ltd.
Milton Keynes UK
UKOW06f0425050316

269651UK00002B/9/P